CABIN STYLE

JANICE BREWSTER

Publications International, Ltd.

Janice Brewster is former editor of *Log Home Living* and *Timber Frame Homes* magazines, where she spent seven years traveling North America and Finland writing about log and timber frame homes and lodges. She is currently a freelance writer living in Alexandria, Virginia. Each summer, Brewster makes a pilgrimage to the woods of Maine to spend time in a cabin that has been in her family for generations. Her first book, *Log Cabins,* was published in 1999.

Copyright © 2001 Publications International, Ltd. All rights reserved. This book may not be reproduced or quoted in whole or in part by any means whatsoever without written permission from:

Louis Weber, CEO
Publications International, Ltd.
7373 North Cicero Avenue
Lincolnwood, Illinois 60712

Permission is never granted for commercial purposes.

Manufactured in China.

8 7 6 5 4 3 2 1

Library of Congress Control Number: 2001087268

ISBN: 0-7853-4892-1

CONTENTS

CABIN STYLE: A CANOPY OF COMFORT

IF YOU HAVEN'T done it since you were a kid, go outside and sit under a tree. Lean back against the strong, warm trunk. Look up at the branches that form the canopy of leaves that shade and protect you. Want to bring that feeling home? You can with a log cabin.

Think of the words "log cabin," and you probably envision a little log house with a shake roof tucked into a grove of trees by a lake. Maybe you see a stone chimney puffing wood smoke. While we often think of a log home's exterior, the interior is what completes a cabin's charm. All kinds of folks succumb to the allure of logs, from new-age pioneers to cutting-edge trendsetters. The styles that decorate log homes are as diverse as the people who live in them. You'll find everything from antiques to contemporary furniture making themselves equally at home.

Maybe you love a particular style—Early American, Arts & Crafts, or Southwestern—and know that a log cabin would be the perfect stage for your style to shine. Or perhaps you'd like to bring a truly classic cabin look—that of the cowboy, rancher, or pioneer—to your current home. Either way, this book will give you acres of ideas for making a log cabin fit your style or for bringing cabin style home.

Whatever your taste, the log or timber frame home is at its heart a comfortable place that glories in the warmth of wood. Look up and you'll see beams and rafters, like the branches of a tree, supporting the roof. The sweet scent and quiet of the forest will embrace you as you walk through the door. Log cabin style is welcoming, honest, and unassuming.

Skilled carpenters and pioneers in the New World felled trees and hewed the logs square. Their homes' logs were lined with chinking and locked together with dovetail corners. **Builder: Hearthstone Homes.**

IN THE BEGINNING

For centuries, people living in the forested regions of Europe and Scandinavia counted on trees for shelter. Their log-building and woodworking skills date back to medieval times. Although the people who fled Europe for the New World left much behind, they did bring along their skills at log crafting.

Residents of countries that had fewer trees, like England, built timbered homes. Instead of creating walls of solid wood, they used their sparse trees more sparingly for the walls' structure and completed the walls with infill made of a plasterlike material. Those who sailed from the British Isles and landed in New England built timber frame homes.

Today, we still celebrate these English, European, and Scandinavian ancestors with homes in Early American and Appalachian styles. For many people, Early American Windsor chairs and pewter candlesticks will never go out of style. Far from the cluttered country look that engulfed the United States in the 1980s, the aesthetic of Early American is spare and dependent on pieces that typify fine woodworking. Colonists would have brought some of these cherished pieces with them on their journeys to the New World.

The shape of the house itself underlines Early American style. These homes have simple forms that include the symmetrical Colonial home, the classic Cape Cod house, and the saltbox. Inside an Early American home, a framed portrait may look down on a four-poster bed topped by a woven coverlet. The home's formal room may feature a gilded Federal-style mirror to reflect the light of a fire crackling in an open hearth. The colors of these rooms can be cool, like Colonial blue, or warm, like oxblood red. And while the New England settlers preferred timber framing to logs for their homes, squared, Appalachian-style logs with wide bands of chinking look just right with this style.

South of New England in Appalachia, settlers built homes of squared logs. They also crafted furniture and wove textiles. The Appalachian-style log cabin embodies American country. Here you'll find rocking chairs on shed-roofed porches, wooden beds layered with scrap quilts, and open stone hearths filled with cast-iron kettles for cooking. The shape of the Appalachian home was also simple. Often porches were tucked under the eaves of a gable roof, and a breezeway, known as a

A loft that might have once been a sleeping space now makes room for a quiet retreat—a place to read or to daydream about the loving hands that first built the log cabin.

"dogtrot," connected two smaller square log buildings and offered a shady spot.

In these Appalachian cabins, kerosene lamplight spilled out onto families who made everything for themselves, from food to rugs to pottery to music. Their hands left behind their spirit, a lure for today's collector. That can-do attitude carried the pioneers to the West, where another log style blossomed.

HANDS TO WORK

Decades after the first Colonists settled in the Northeast, the Shakers, a religious sect that fled persecution in England, landed in New York state. As the religion gained converts,

Shaker communities formed in New England, Kentucky, and Indiana. As part of their communal life, Shakers crafted furniture, baskets, and other items for sale. Although the Shakers' buildings were not made of logs, the style they created is well-suited for a home made of clean-lined logs or timber framing.

To remove clutter from living spaces, the Shakers perfected the craft of cabinetry. Wooden pegs on walls provided a perch for the assorted items that even simple life requires, like chairs, hats, and tools. The Shakers stripped away unnecessary ornamentation in their quest to create items that fulfilled specific purposes. Their furniture, while not overly carved or

turned, gains its beauty from simple form, color, and the beauty of wood grain.

Because the Shakers believed in celibacy, their numbers have diminished to just a handful today, increasing the scarcity and value of their work. Reproductions enable all who enjoy clean lines and simple beauty to bring the Shaker look home. Ladder-back chairs and rockers, trestle tables, and tall chests of drawers exude Shaker style. Bandboxes and woven baskets are the perfect accessories. The Shakers also used color—typically red, blue, and chrome yellow—in their meetinghouses, homes, and furnishings.

MORE IS MORE

In stark contrast to Shaker style, Americans at the end of the 1800s loved opulence. The mass-produced furnishings and accessories manufactured during the Industrial Revolution fed their hunger. Ornate furniture topped with layers of silk and velvet and accessorized with bric-a-brac became the fashion. Oriental rugs decorated the floors, and heavy drapery dripping with fringe festooned tall windows.

By the end of the century in settled regions of the United States, log homes were out of fashion. New methods of framing homes with sawn, dimensional lumber and the invention of mass-produced nails meant that most people built wood-framed homes trimmed with decorative woodwork. In fact, some people living in log homes at the time sheathed their outdated log walls in clapboard and paneling. Still, the Victorian look can successfully be brought to a log cabin, especially one with squared logs that offer a smooth canvas for hanging the multitude of paintings, mirrors, and knickknacks that are the hallmarks of this style.

For their abundant luxury, Victorian-style dining rooms and bedrooms are always in fashion, no matter what the architectural backdrop. Chandeliers that illuminate a dining table draped in heavy damask or lace and set with china, silver, and crystal elevate meals to special events. In the bedroom, the femininity of Victorian style makes for sweet dreams.

BACK TO THE HAND

Not everyone loved Victorian style, however. Some found the ornate, garish, and machine-made goods shoddy. These people longed for a return to the Middle Ages, when fine artisans learned their crafts through a guild system. Thus, in the early 1900s, the Arts & Crafts movement was born.

Gustav Stickley, a furniture maker from New York state, personified the movement. To set the stage for his honest, handcrafted furniture, Stickley advocated a "sturdy and friendly type of architecture." In 1908, Stickley built a log farmhouse on 600 acres in rural New Jersey and dubbed it Craftsman Farms.

Inside a typical Arts & Crafts–style home, dark wood prevailed. Carved wainscoting stretched from the floor to eye level, and diamond panes

Squared logs make a rich backdrop for Victorian style. Heavy, dark wood furnishings contrast with the honey-hued logs, which, in turn, complement the upholstery in shades of peach.

A pair of massive log posts form the boundaries of a seating area around the fire. Classic Arts & Crafts–style armchairs offer their simple comfort by the hearth. **Builder: Alpine Log Homes, Inc.**

or rectilinear designs ornamented windows and doors. Near the center of the home, an inglenook surrounded the fireplace, which may have been accented by handmade tiles. Richly grained wood floors were topped with rugs patterned after William Morris's textiles.

The furnishings produced at the time differed sharply from their Victorian predecessors. The linear style of Stickley's chairs and settees shrugged off the baroque ornamentation the Victorians loved. Like the Shakers, the crafts-people of this age relied on the wood's own beauty and the skill of their hands to make furniture both beautiful and comfortable.

Everything for the home was to be handmade. Light fixtures were made of copper and topped with mica shades. Pottery was thrown by hand. Woven curtains, table runners, and bed linens wore simple embellishments of stylized leaves and flowers. The colors were muted and natural.

Authentic and reproduction Arts & Crafts furniture and accessories look right at home with logs. Like log crafting, they echo the work of the hand, and their colors are the colors of the forest, suiting them perfectly for log and timber rooms.

WEALTH IN THE WILDERNESS

At the height of the Victorian age, before the Arts & Crafts move-ment blossomed, the barons of the Industrial Revolution discovered the outdoors. Tales of abundant fish and game and the curing power of fresh air lured America's wealthiest families to the Adirondack forests of northern New York. There they bought up acres of land and planned for compounds of self-sufficient getaways.

Many of the compounds began as sites for permanent tents, but they quickly outgrew their rough origins. The goal was to make the wilderness luxurious, while maintaining a patina of rusticity. Small log buildings soon clustered around a main lodge. Mother Nature served as interior designer: Birch bark lined walls and ceilings, twigs set in mosaic patterns trimmed

windows and doors, crooked branches became stair railings, and stone piled up into founda-tions and chimneys. The lodges built in this style became known as the Great Camps.

Despite their remote locations, the owners of the Great Camps prided themselves on offering their guests every amenity, from electricity and indoor plumbing to bowling alleys and chapels. The furnishings of the camps reflected the period when they were built. Early log camps were furnished in ornate Victorian style. As the century turned, however, Great Camp style veered toward Arts & Crafts, with Stickley-style rockers pulled up to stone fireplaces. No matter what the style, the evidence of the artisan's hand was everywhere. Beds were fashioned from hand-peeled and waxed

If you're going to be snowed in, there's no more charm-ing place to be than in this log cabin. Delicate birch bark balances the weight of the massive arched fireplace and echoes the home's furniture and loft railings. **Builder: Alpine Log Homes, Inc.**

branches, and handwoven baskets formed lampshades. Local craftspeople forged ironwork for the camps' light fixtures, hardware, and fireplace screens.

SPREADING THE WEALTH

For decades, the Great Camps spread their influence across the United States. Their impact, and visions of Old World hunting lodges, has evolved into the lodge style that many of today's log cabin owners bring to their homes. Logs used in this style can be round or flat, or timber framing can be used. Whatever shape the wood takes and the bigger the logs or timbers, the better a backdrop for this truly masculine style of decor.

No lodge-style home is complete without a massive fireplace, preferably built of stone. Wood accents in the home's furnishings, floor, and trim may be dark and heavy. Picture a billiard room or library designed for gentlemen smoking cigars and talking politics.

The colors of this style are dark and muted tones of the natural colors that decorated the Great Camps: moss green, deep reds, and nutmeg browns. The deep colors also offer a range of textures, from leather to brocade to velvet. Antler chandeliers light these rooms with style. Of course, with a nod to the hunting tradition on which the style is based, animal mounts and trophies are a must.

WESTWARD EXPANSION

Log cabins sheltered the pioneers as they settled the frontier. A man could build a log cabin with his own two hands. Inside, his wife would make the place a home with quilts, rag rugs, and maybe one or two good pieces of furniture that made the trip from back East. Some pioneers abandoned their log cabins as soon as they had the wherewithal to build a frame house. Others, like the ranchers of the West, built their log homes for the generations.

Care was taken with log ranch houses to peel the logs and perhaps shape them to interlock with each other. If round logs were stacked up, the gaps between them were filled with chinking of horsehair and mud or plaster. A wide porch gave the ranchers room to wash up before they came inside.

Today, ranch-style log cabins endure as American icons. With a stone fireplace or an iron woodstove at its center, the cabin on the ranch is casual and utilitarian. Navajo rugs or cowhides might gussy up the wide-planked wood floors. The furnishings are oversized and comfortable, with a rocking chair stationed at the hearth and leather armchairs and sofas nearby for relaxing after a day of riding the range. Log beds covered with woolen Native American blankets provide rest for the weary. Above it all hang chandeliers made of entwined antlers or forged iron. Saddles, boots, lariats, and spurs hung on the wall remind modern-day ranchers of their roots—a lifestyle captured in Remington's bronze sculptures, which also look right at home in the log cabin ranch.

ON THE LIGHT SIDE

Just as the wealthy Eastern establishment flocked to the Adirondacks at the turn of the century, a few decades later they began looking for outdoor adventure farther afield. To cater to these elite with visions of cattle drives and buffalo hunts, the dude ranch gained rapid popularity in the early 1900s.

Many dude ranches were spruced up for their city slicker patrons. The person who created what is termed Cowboy High Style was Thomas Molesworth, a furniture maker from Cody, Wyoming, who accepted several commissions to furnish Western ranches and hotels. His furnishings depict the Western lifestyle in romanticized glory. He peeled and polished fir and lodgepole pine branches to frame his furniture and upholstered the pieces in brightly colored leather or Chimayo weavings. Wood burls and brass tacks were used as accents, and silhouettes of lone cowboys or Indian braves often decorated seat backs and headboards. Molesworth also fashioned special furnishings like bars and writing desks at which the dudes could pen postcards to send home.

Lighting for the dude ranch buildings came from iron or wagon wheel fixtures. The ranch's textiles followed tradition with brightly striped Hudson's Bay blankets and Navajo rugs. The accessories used to complete the setting included spurs, saddles, boots, and bows and arrows, while art on the walls depicted the fabled life of the cowboy singing under the stars and driving cattle across the great open spaces.

The furnishings, which followed the Arts & Crafts tradition, made the dude ranches comfortable for their posh guests, while still providing a somewhat primitive, rustic feel. Today, authentic Molesworth furnishings are highly coveted, and several Western companies craft reproductions for those who'd like to bring Cowboy High Style home.

The Cowboys and Indians theme can even be carried to its kitschy extreme with framed

Western style shows through in this cozy log home, which displays a mountaineer's snowshoes, a Navajo rug, and a Southwestern-style sofa table and kiva ladder. Builder: Rocky Mountain Log Homes.

Above: *Masculine lodge style pervades this impressive log home. Generous chairs, including two fashioned of moose horns, and a deep sofa offer a place to sit back and swap tales of the hunt.* Architect: Charles Cunniffe Architects.

Cowboy and Indian legends fuel the romance of the Old West. In this home, a bedroom glories in that romantic tradition. A bold Native American design spans the floor, while broncos buck across the beds. Builder: Rocky Mountain Log Homes.

Western movie posters and pony-skin bar stools with cowboy boots for legs. Whether it's campy or sincere, your collection of Western memorabilia will fit right in to a log cabin of any style.

SOUTH AND WEST

The desert Southwest offered its inhabitants few trees. There, precious timbers were used to create roof and ceiling structures to support the heavy roofs of adobe homes. Today, logs can be imported to these desert regions, and rounded, light-colored logs make a beautiful setting for decor inspired by the Southwest.

Southwestern style is a mixture of Spanish and Native American influences. Traditionally, small windows, thick adobe walls, and tiled floors

The work of Native Americans of the Southwest decorates this room, including such masterpieces as woven blankets and rugs, pottery, and modern artwork. A boot-shape lamp represents the cowboy's role in the Southwest. **Builder: Alpine Log Homes, Inc.**

helped keep homes cool in the desert heat. Today, terra cotta tiles and adobe accents make a wonderful, earthy complement to the warm wood tones of logs.

Southwestern-style furnishings may be carved Spanish Colonial wood tables and case pieces that remind us of centuries-old missions. The cruciform is repeated in carvings, recalling the influence of the missionaries. Some of these pieces wear a coat of paint in the colors of the sand, sunset, and sky. On the floor or walls, brightly colored woven rugs and serapes add dashes of color. Beehive-style fireplaces take the chill off desert nights, and handmade pottery reflects the talent of native-born peoples. Mexican silver adds sparkle, while adobe is sculpted into soft, rounded archways.

SUMMER PLACES

Log cabins and summer vacations go together. In recreation areas across the country, from the woods of New England and the Northeast to the lakes of the Midwest, families built log cabins as escapes from their urban and suburban homes. The log style of these cottages and cabins varies from round to square, but it typically forms small, utilitarian buildings.

The basics of cottage style are comfort and practicality. Inside you'll find wood floors, sometimes painted a cottage gray. Walk through a screen door, and you step out onto a porch—a must for enjoying summer twilights. In the

Cottage style, a close cousin to the summer camp look, makes this living room cheerful and cozy. A lively braided rug adds even more spice to the mix of patterns in the upholstery and window treatments. **Builder: Alpine Log Homes, Inc.**

kitchen, you'll find painted cabinetry or just open shelves stacked with Grandma's everyday dishes. The furnishings of cottage style are unpretentious and include slipcovered armchairs, well-loved wicker, or a set of simple painted chairs gathered around a large pine table. Lighting comes from humble fixtures of tin or metal, and vintage table lamps cast a soft light on this nostalgic style. Chenille spreads and scrap quilts top off the beds, while faded chintz florals and awning-striped cushions add even more comfort. Signs of the outdoors are at home here, too. Wildflowers in a Fiestaware vase or watercolors of lakeside views remind the owners of nature's beauty just outside the door.

Take cottage style, subtract its feminine wiles, and you have the look of the summer camp. These manly retreats, built to house hunters, fishermen, and summer campers, are more rustic than their cottage counterparts. Here, rounded log walls give a rustic background for simple, utilitarian furnishings. Tools of the trade—guidebooks, maps, fishing poles and lures, rifles and mounts—work as accessories. Light may come from kerosene lamps or an antler chandelier, and a black iron woodstove dries wet clothes and crackles as fish stories are swapped. The kitchen is the place to clean fish and make strong coffee. It may be outfitted with vintage utensils like graniteware kettles and cast-iron skillets for frying up the day's catch.

THE CONTEMPORARY CABIN

While many log cabin styles glory in the patina of age, modern and contemporary decorating schemes fit right in to log cabins, too. Lovers of the clean, sparse lines of contemporary looks may choose a light-colored log or timber frame to enhance the style. Wide windows with no divisions carry out the modern look and open the cabin to the outdoors. The furnishings may be inspired by Scandinavian blond wood and chrome classics.

The contemporary home takes on an open floor plan. Sleek touches add their edge, from metal spiral staircases and railings to glass block. A fireplace is still the center of the home, but instead of being rustic and ornate, it's stripped to its essence of firebox and hearth. Lighting can also add contemporary flair. Recessed lights, track lighting, and tapered torchères add drama to the space as they spotlight log trusses and

An eclectic-style cabin provides the opportunity to mix and match items from many different styles. Native American weavings, Western bronze statues, and Early American quilted throw pillows create a nice combination in this living room. **Builder: Alpine Log Homes, Inc.**

ceiling beams. In the kitchen, stainless-steel appliances reinforce contemporary style. The primary colors of a Mondrian painting or a wash of neutrals all carry the look, and accessories are carefully edited.

ALL TOGETHER NOW

Of course the log cabin's easy attitude accepts a mixture of styles. If your taste tends toward the eclectic, you'll find logs accommodating. No-fuss country style combined with Shaker simplicity and contemporary precision leads to homes that follow no set rules; instead, they cater to their owners' wide-ranging interests. The casual eclectic style works in any wood home, regardless of the style of timbers or log work.

A few classics remain in this style: The hearth as the heart of the home and the appreciation of the handmade. Colors may be muted and earthy or warm and neutral. Texture, in velvet, chenille, and leather, is key to the casual eclectic look and provides another layer of comfort. Accessories include pottery, metal-framed mirrors, and lit candles, and cast-iron accents abound in drapery hardware, drawer pulls, and light fixtures. The furnishings may be dark wood or painted in the tradition of the cottage.

So, whether you desire a decor that looks as if it just stepped out of the pages of a history book or you prefer a sleek, contemporary design with all of today's amenities, the log cabin can easily embrace all the styles you love.

THE BEST OF YESTERDAY

WITH TREES as far as the eye could see, it's no wonder that pioneers, trappers, loggers, and mountain men used logs to build shelter from the elements. What passed for interior decor in these rustic cabins was either made by hand or brought from home—whether home was across the ocean in Europe or back East in the first colonies. Log cabins embrace fond memories of days past. From the solid woodworking of Early American pieces to the ornate embellishments of the Victorian era to the quarter-sawn oak pieces of Gustav Stickley—whatever your heart desires, that style will fit in a log cabin. Although its roots are buried in other lands, we've adopted the log cabin as an American icon. To give your historic decor a ring of truth, be sure you include items that embody the spirit of Americans and the work of their hands.

Left: *Arts & Crafts style, which first blossomed in England, made its way to the United States in the early 1900s. Its abundant use of handmade wood furniture makes this style a natural in log cabins.* **Builder: Alpine Log Homes, Inc. Right:** *The Arts & Crafts movement was influenced by the style and crafting of the Middle Ages. This library table with a leather top reveals that medieval influence.* **Manufacturer: Stickley.**

EARLY AMERICAN CHARM

FOLKS OFTEN FALL IN LOVE with log cabins because they show how life used to be. We just can't resist these life-size souvenirs of our scrappy pioneer past. Logs raised to shelter a settler's family still make a cozy home today. So whether your cabin is brand new or centuries old, you can give it the look of Early America with Colonial-style furnishings and accessories, as pictured here. Choose light fixtures that disguise today's electricity with yesterday's style, and add matte-textured colors on door and window trim. To continue the look, use logs that are hand-peeled or hewn square. Underneath it all, wood plank flooring in a variety of widths is not only a beautiful choice but will stand up to years of use. Play up beautifully functional handmade items, and you're well on your way to creating Early American style in your own log cabin.

Opposite: *The beauty of an old home is the way it shows its age—from the well-trod steps of a staircase to its primitive doors. Here, cherished possessions from the past—such as a quilt, a handwoven rug, and wooden bowls—reinforce the home's authenticity.*

Above: *A pioneer's life left little room for luxuries. A simple white curtain strung across a window on twine and an electric candle burning on the sill soften the rough look and feel of a settler's cabin. Evergreen boughs and holly berries add cheer to long winter nights.*

Right: *Primitive furniture sets the scene in this kitchen. The simple table, desk, and benches have withstood years of use. Wood's warmth appears throughout the room, from a hand-hewn beam above to a host of wooden containers, including a barrel, a firkin, and a collection of bandboxes.*

Victorian style shines in the dining room, where rich table linens and the best china set the scene for special occasions. No Victorian home would be complete without stained glass sparkling in the windows.

Wicker is essential to Victorian style. Here, a wicker coffee table complements a floral sofa, while candlelight and the soft glow of milk-glass-shaded lamps heighten the room's romantic feel.

The focal point of this room is the richly decorated fireplace. Screened for the summer, the firebox is surrounded by a detailed mantel topped with a wide mirror. Swags of flowers adorn the mantel and the wide windows. **Builder: Sisson Log Homes, Inc.**

VICTORIAN SENSIBILITY

VICTORIAN STYLE brings a woman's touch to log cabins. And while the style is certainly not rustic, logs do form a warm background for the many layers of ornamentation. When Victorian style peaked, the 20th century was approaching and bringing with it innovations like gaslights and machine-made furniture. Homemade gave way to store-bought. To bring the Victorian look to your log cabin, be sure to include the hallmarks of this style—florals, lace, and ornate furniture. Display collections of gilt frames or porcelain on tabletops or walls, and choose upholstery in rich tones and floral patterns. Underline the style with luxurious Oriental carpets and light fixtures and lamps of the period, and opt for deep wood tones to play up the style's rich look.

Left: *Rich colors make the sleeping loft even more cozy. A Pendleton blanket tops the wood-framed bed, and pastoral paintings depict a nature lover's view of the woods.*

A collection of vintage sports equipment is on display at the cabin's door. Old skis and tiny snowshoes pair up with a fisherman's creel and hat.

PRESERVING THE PAST

A CHILDHOOD FANTASY, an adult sanctuary, and a salute to the pioneer past are all rolled into this one small cabin. Warmed by a stacked-stone fireplace and decorated with souvenirs from yesteryear, this pint-size place offers the perfect spot to get away from the hustle and bustle of modern life. Among the cabin's layers of furnishings and accessories, you'll find tokens of the pioneer pursuits of trapping, hunting, and fishing: mounted trophies, pelts, rods, creels, and snowshoes. All are tempered by the feminine touch provided by layers of hand-pieced quilts and woven blankets. The owner's collection of vintage wildlife paintings looks just right against the log walls, with their heavy bands of primitive white chinking. Even if you don't know how to quilt or never fish for your supper, this cabin takes you in and makes you at home.

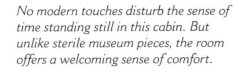

No modern touches disturb the sense of time standing still in this cabin. But unlike sterile museum pieces, the room offers a welcoming sense of comfort.

JOINT PRECISION

THE ARTS & CRAFTS MOVEMENT, which sprang up in England and caught hold in the United States in the early 1900s, glorified the work of the craftsperson. Simple lines, handwoven textiles, and handcrafted furniture formed a stark contrast to the ornamented and baroque interiors of the Victorian era. Arts & Crafts, or Mission, style is quite at home in log cabins. Both glow with natural warmth, and both play up the inherent beauty of wood. In this home, handcrafted square logs are carefully stacked and locked together with dovetail corners. The same attention to precise wood joinery shows in the Stickley-style furnishings found throughout the house. To carry out the look, light fixtures, window panes, stair railings, and more exhibit the simple geometric patterns that are so common to the Arts & Crafts look.

Above: *Light fixtures with colored glass shades and geometric patterns continue the Arts & Crafts theme. Even the windows, with their rectilinear panes, echo the style. In the corner, a chest of drawers shows Japan's influence on the style.*

Right: *Arts & Crafts–style homes of the early 1900s often featured a hearth at their centers. This contemporary home draws from that era, boasting a soapstone masonry heater that radiates warmth from the heart of the open floor plan.*

Opposite: *A timbered dormer creates a cozy nook in the home's loft. Rich leather upholsters the Stickley-style rocker and chair, while kilim-covered throw pillows and a patterned rug add a touch of color.* **Architect: Jean Steinbrecher. Builder: Unique Log & Timber Works.**

THE SIMPLE LIFE

SIMPLE LINES and design that showcases the beauty of wood are the hallmarks of Shaker style. This log cabin reveals that same purity of form in its timber framing, clean-lined staircase, and custom kitchen cabinetry. While the furnishings are somewhat softer and rounder than classic Shaker pieces, they do show a love of wood and its organic form. Even with these refined elements, the home retains the rustic feel of a settler's cabin. For example, the stout, hand-peeled logs that create the walls and ceiling beams could have been felled by a pioneer's ax. Twiggy furniture and a chandelier fashioned from shed antlers reveal the beauty in nature's forms. Native American rugs and a wagon wheel light fixture in the loft bring a touch of the Old West into this home steeped in tradition.

Above: *A Shaker-style four-poster bed is paired with rustic twig chairs that curl up to the master bedroom's stone hearth.*

Right: *The rough and the refined go together in this home's dining area. Round log posts and beams are topped by trusses of finely finished timbers.*
Opposite: *The dirt floor of the settler's cabin is upgraded to stone throughout this log cabin. Stone appears on the countertops and backsplash, too, making a cool counterpoint to the warm wood cabinets.* **Builder: Spring Creek Timber Construction.**

VICTORIAN VARIETY

Tʜɪs ᴄᴀʙɪɴ reveals its owners' wide-ranging tastes as well as their affection for Victorian style. The living room has a Great Camps feel, thanks to Victorian-style lighting and patterned upholstery, rustic twiggy tables, and the more masculine touches of a leather armchair and mounted deer trophy. Everything in the room is designed for comfort and ease: A library ladder scales a well-stocked bookcase, and a fireplace crackles with warmth in the evening. The dining room, too, follows in the tradition of the Victorian Great Camps, with rustic furniture and antler accessories surrounded by lavish luxury. The cabin's oversize windows feature multiple panes to lend the charm of an older log home, while the vaulted ceilings make the space feel modern and informal.

Above: *The cabin's dining room would have been the toast of the Great Camps. Its rustic furniture is accented with a richly framed wildlife painting and underlined by a thick Oriental rug.*

Right: *While Victorian-inspired bedding layers the bed, the bedroom offers elements in a range of styles, from the twiggy table and birch bark mirror to the contemporary lines of the artwork and window blinds.*

Opposite: *Partition walls topped with a frieze of branches separate this living room from the home's welcoming entry. On the sofa table, a model canoe echoes the scene carved in the mantel.* **Builder:** Town and Country Cedar Homes.

WARMTH OF SPIRIT

GERMAN IMMIGRANTS who settled in the Hill Country of central Texas in the mid-1800s quickly set to work building homes of squared logs accented with rock work. This Texas pioneer homestead, which now serves as a bed-and-breakfast cottage, glories in its roots and invites visitors to spend time in an era when central heating was a fireplace in every room and a home security system was a shotgun hung above the mantel. Here, the feeling of the 19th century is preserved but with no museum stuffiness. As this picture-perfect home shows, the key to historic style is getting the details right. From artwork to accessories to window treatments, take your cue from yesterday's trends to create a log cabin that has both historic charm and today's comfort.

Right: *This room pays homage to settlers who arrived in a new land, built their own homes, wove their own bed covers, and braided their own rugs. Items made by skilled hands are displayed throughout the bedroom, adding to the space's warmth of spirit.*

Above: *In a settler's cabin, space was precious. To conserve it, a narrow staircase winds its way up to the sleeping area. A small window, accented with deep red trim, sheds light on the stairs, with help from a simple wall sconce.*

Opposite: *A cheerful fire lures guests to the living room during the chilly nights and winters in Texas Hill Country. A comfortable cushioned settee, a bright blue hutch, and warm Oriental carpets make this homestead homey.*

FUNCTIONAL BEAUTY

WHILE VICTORIAN and Art Noveau styles made abundant use of curves and curlicues, Arts & Crafts style favored the straight line for its simple purity. Function was of the utmost importance in furnishings, and ornamentation was kept to a minimum. These Arts & Crafts values perfectly complement the timber frame, or post-and-beam, home, like this one. Squared timbers echo the straight lines, and their function as the home's structural skeleton dictates their form. Heavy wood timber framing can also be paired with log walls to create homes with soaring interior spaces. In these cases, you'll want to emphasize furnishings and accessories with weight and mass. Spindly pieces tend to shrink in these large, vaulted rooms, so you'll need furnishings that can hold their own.

Opposite: *The pattern of straight railings on the open staircase is echoed in the Arts & Crafts–style table in this open great room. A pair of substantial dark wicker chairs fits right in to the decorating scheme.* **Builder: Riverbend Timber Framing.**

Above: *A lowered ceiling and a rich Oriental rug make the dining room intimate and warm. A design inspired by Frank Lloyd Wright plays on the hanging pendant light fixture and is repeated in the banks of tall windows.*

Left: *Bead board cabinetry in the kitchen continues the pattern of vertical lines started by the bar stools. Glass-front cabinets carry the same rectilinear design as the window panes.*

Above: *Even the difficult life of a settler and rancher left some time to sit on a porch swing, listening to the cattle and enjoying the cool night air.*

Opposite: *Wide barn boards top the ceiling joists and panel one wall in this log cabin. A Shaker-style bed topped with a quilt oversees a pair of casual overstuffed armchairs.*

A bent willow chair pulled up to a rustic table is the perfect spot to have breakfast and plan the day's adventures. Throw pillows covered with flowers encourage guests to linger awhile over coffee.

THROUGH THE YEARS

EARLY SETTLERS used what nature gave them to build shelters for their families. In some areas of the country, it was forests filled with trees; in other areas, farm fields were cleared of stones, which could then be used for houses and barns. Often, wood and stone were used together to create enduring homes with a pleasant mix of warm and cool elements. This home captures the feel of a settler's cabin, then layers it with treasures from many eras. Bent willow chairs sit on an Oriental carpet, while Victorian lamps shed light on farm tools left over from a pioneer past. To further the mix-and-match feel, feminine florals meet brash cowboy memorabilia like boots and chaps. All are comfortable together in this cozy cabin of wood and stone.

FIT FOR A KING

AT ONE TIME log cabins were associated with the hardscrabble life of the pioneer or cowboy. Today, a log cabin can make room for every luxury, including crystal chandeliers, fine paintings, and cherished antiques. More of a castle than a cabin, this log home sparkles with opulence that a pioneer could only dream of. From its mountainside perch, this ranch combines the elegance of a French boudoir with the dark masculinity of a Victorian drawing room. The style starts with richly patterned rugs and ornate light fixtures; antique furnishings are then added for a touch of elegance. Finally, yards of luxurious fabrics, like brocades, silks, and velvets, upholster the furniture, drape the windows, and dress the beds. With the lighting of the grand fireplaces and the sparkling chandeliers, the home's stunning ambience is complete.

Left: *A European fireplace warms the bedroom, while wide windows look out over a uniquely American vista of mountains and valleys. Sumptuous linens and drapes dress the space with grace.*

Delicate crystal and china are set on a table built for a king or, at least, landed gentry. The chairs' seats are upholstered in leather and their legs are finished with ornamental turns.

A framed cowboy painting brings the New World to this Old World–style library. Plush upholstery and deep armchairs make the room a perfect gentleman's hideaway.

BACK TO THE LAND

ALTHOUGH A PIONEER'S LIFE was hard, it was played out against the beautiful and always changing landscape of the frontier itself. This homeowner set out to fill the cabin with pieces of the period to create a space free from modern distractions—a place to dwell on the peacefulness of a life spent close to the land. The cabin was built around 1915, and its furnishings are a reflection of that era. A cookstove provided both heat and meals, while an icebox helped preserve food. The furnishings are straightforward and simple: a pair of straight chairs, a rocker, metal bedsteads, and a sofa for quiet times. When darkness falls, kerosene lanterns are lighted, and life continues inside the cabin much as it has for almost a century.

Above right: *A trunk is pulled up to the foot of one of the metal-framed beds, which are topped with snowy white coverlets to stay in line with the cabin's simple decor.*
Right: *The wood cookstove remains at the center of the cabin to offer both heat and home cookin'. A hide rug helps take the chill off the floor.*

Opposite: *A gate leg table opens to make room for two or more to eat, then folds down to make more space in the room. Small windows provide light inside during the day.* Designer: Sandra Elizabeth Clinger, ASID, Lifestyle Interior Design.

Right: *While homeowners in the early 1900s never dreamed of commercial ranges, dishwashers, and refrigerators, a modern kitchen can look right at home in a period-style house. Here, handforged hardware on handcrafted cabinetry blends the kitchen with the home's Arts & Crafts decor.*

A stained-glass masterpiece at the front door makes a striking first impression. A table lamp with a mica shade lights the Stickley sideboard and sets the stage for an authentic Arts & Crafts interior.

ARTS & CRAFTS MASTERPIECE

Arts & Crafts style, with its subtle luxury, informality, and durability, is the perfect match for a well-loved log home that offers its owners warmth, good looks, and comfort. The key to reproducing any style in your log cabin is to pay attention to the details of that style. Items that may at first seem inconsequential, like light fixtures and door knobs, can make or break the look. Proponents of the Arts & Crafts movement believed that every item in the home must be either beautiful or functional. Items that didn't pass that test were just clutter to be cleared away. Today, comfort is the ultimate function, and this home takes advantage of that, with richly upholstered Stickley-style furnishings in the great room and plenty of modern conveniences in the kitchen.

Opposite: *A verdigris light fixture illuminates this great room and shows the Asian influence on Arts & Crafts design. The Stickley-style chairs and sofa are a perfect match for the finely finished wood mantel.* **Builder: Alpine Log Homes, Inc.**

Right: *From the looks of this kitchen, you'd never guess that time hadn't stopped 80 years ago. Meals prepared on a wood cookstove are brought lovingly to the simple plank table.*

Above: *Despite the many daily chores of pioneer life, some artistic soul found time to paint scenes from farm life on these cast-off saw blades. An iron candlestick and old crank phone are quaint reminders of the past.*

HANDS TO WORK

NOW, IN A TIME when we purchase just about everything we need and search for ways to spend our free time, it's hard to imagine the life of the pioneer. Quite literally "homemakers," these settlers used their hands to create what they needed to live. This home celebrates the skilled hands that turned these items of necessity into art. Braided rugs and handmade quilts decorate a home built of logs cut and stacked by hand. The cabin's accessories, such as the loom and crosscut saw, handmade chairs, and forged iron lamps, show that our ancestors' homes were seldom idle. Trim at the doors and the wide plank floors are straightforward and nothing fancy. This home is quite simply shelter for the family and the warm center of its life.

Opposite: *A bentwood swing is the whimsical centerpiece of this living room. Antique pieces, including the buggy seat that serves as a coffee table, are warm reminders of the past.*

LAYERS OF HISTORY

THE SPIRIT OF AMERICANA shows in the details of this home, which is topped by rustic hand-peeled log beams. Shades of Colonial red and blue underline the historic style and combine the character and strength of antique pieces with the comfort of today. Small details, such as a pewter plate on the mantel, rich wood wainscoting, and metal light fixtures, call the past to mind. With Early American style as a base, the homeowners layered on furnishings and accessories from other eras, including Arts & Crafts–style chairs, tables, and lighting, and vintage summer camp accessories like the fishing-themed throw pillows, campy signs, and pair of classic valises. Taken together, they create an all-American style.

Right: *Rustic log beams accent the lower level of this home. A bed draped with a quilt pieced in patriotic red, white, and blue is just steps away from the warmth of the fire.* **Builder: Snow Country Construction. Designer: Warren Sheets Design.**

Above: *Old world carvings cloak this kitchen's modern amenities with folksy charm. Above, a woodland-inspired chandelier hangs over the island. Simple crocks top the cabinets, and stone paves the floor in rustic simplicity.*

Right: *This bedroom offers all the comforts of today, from plump cushions and a thick patterned rug to a bath suite tiled in Colonial blue. Drapes gathered at the corners of an antique four-poster bed and a wing chair and bench with turned spindles provide touches of the past.*

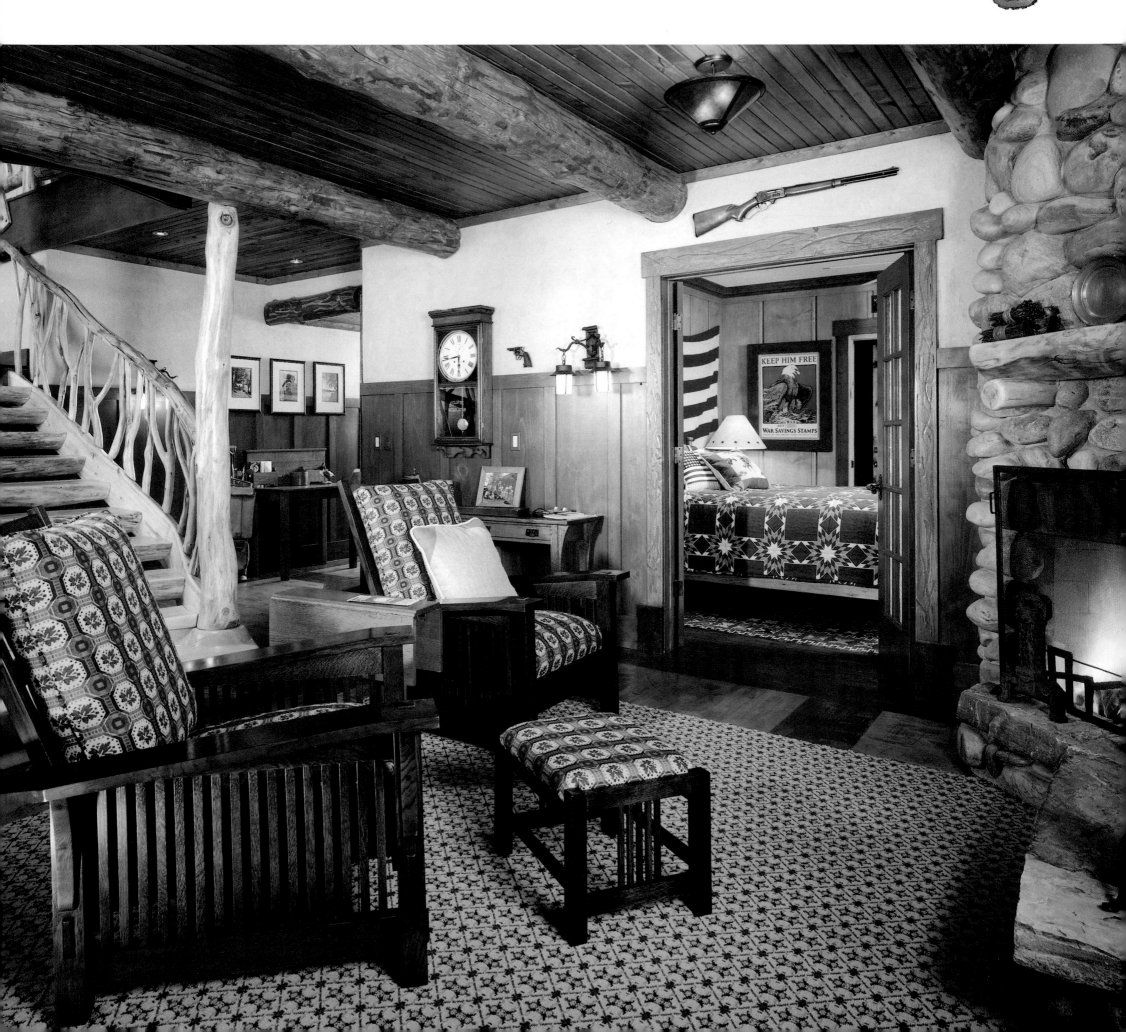

HISTORICAL VALUE

IF YOU WANT a home that overflows with historic character, a log cabin is the perfect place to start. The very walls of your home will tell of days gone by. With the backdrop set, you're ready to layer on furniture and accessories that will cement your home's vintage style. You might choose the starkly beautiful lines of Shaker furniture or the classic shape of traditional Early American Windsor chairs to set the tone. Your choice of floor covering—from a Victorian Oriental beauty to a rug braided from fabric scraps—will underline your cabin's mood. Lighting, too, sparks historic style, so choose your lamps and fixtures carefully, whether it's bronze table lamps for an Arts & Crafts–style home or a pewter chandelier to reinforce an Early American look.

The rich colors and ornate design of this table lamp fit right in to Victorian style. Leaves and berries circle the lamp's shade in a garland motif. **Manufacturer: Quoizel.**

Gustav Stickley designed his Spindle Arm Chair in 1905. This reproduction combines delicate vertical spindles and a patterned seat cushion with the chair's strong, simple lines. **Manufacturer: Stickley.**

A Shaker-style sofa table reveals the golden warmth of wood. This piece is surprisingly elegant in its simplicity. **Manufacturer: Plow & Hearth.**

In an Early American cabin, nothing was ever wasted. Old clothes and blankets were torn into strips and braided into colorful rugs. This oval rug carries on the tradition. **Manufacturer: Plow & Hearth.**

Pottery, especially pieces drenched in earthy and aqueous colors, was highlighted in Arts & Crafts style. Here, aqua blue ceramic tile tops a reproduction end table. **Manufacturer: Stickley.**

This prairie-style clock, an Arts & Crafts–style classic, is reproduced in Mission oak. The clock's design dates back to 1910. **Manufacturer: Stickley.**

High-backed chairs and benches, like the brick red bench pictured here, captured and reflected the warmth of the fire in Early American and Shaker homes. **Manufacturer: Plow & Hearth.**

This book pedestal bears the mark of Roycroft, a community of craftspeople who created furniture, lighting, and home accessories in New York in the early 1900s. **Manufacturer: Stickley.**

THE GREAT CAMPS

WHAT WAS a New York socialite to do in the late 1800s? Summer in the city was so hot and stifling. Gamely, she packed her steamer trunks and spent July at an oceanfront mansion in Newport. Then in August, she boarded a train bound for the Adirondacks, where evergreens fringe the shores of shimmering lakes. In the Adirondack forests, families like the Vanderbilts and the Rockefellers entertained at the "Great Camps," sprawling compounds of log buildings with rustic exteriors and modern conveniences. Most Great Camps were built of unpeeled logs and trimmed with split branches and bark. Inside, guests made themselves comfortable in log beds built by local craftspeople and around dining tables set with meals prepared by servants. The great outdoors was the main attraction, and the decor reminded guests of their surroundings. Great Camp style, with its twig furnishings, mounted animal trophies, and Adirondack chairs, is now a log cabin classic. The lodge look owes its start to both the Great Camps and the baronial hunting lodges of the Old World. Heavy European furnishings and dark colors surrounded by massive log walls complete the lodge-style look.

Left: *A historic ranch in Montana creates the perfect spot for a new log cabin that follows in the lodge tradition. Oversize furnishings make room for all to enjoy the large, open gathering room.* **Builder: Rocky Mountain Log Homes. Above:** *This clock showcases a timeless admiration for the beauty of nature. Pinecones, twigs, and bark set in a simple form create a memorable piece.* **Manufacturer: Whispering Pines.**

Above: Hanging above a grand antique cabinet, which makes room for special-occasion china, a faux deer trophy pokes fun at the home's hunting lodge style.

HANDCRAFTED CHARM

THE GREAT CAMPS of the Adirondacks played up the romance of the log cabin. The owners of these compounds refined the typical fishing camp by adding charming windows, comfortable chairs—and running water. During the long winters, the owners commissioned their off-duty guides to make furniture for the camps. These craftspeople obliged, filling the summer homes with gnarled chairs and tables topped with twig inlay and accented with chip carvings. The pieces echoed the forest surroundings and had a style all their own. Although this home doesn't follow directly in the footsteps of the Great Camps, it does reveal their influence in its hand-peeled log trusses and attention-grabbing stone fireplace. Burled wood and primitive carvings accent the kitchen's cabinetry and counter, while handcrafted logs repeat the warm, masculine tones of the home's decor.

Above: While the owners of the Great Camps had chefs on their staffs, most of today's log cabin owners enjoy cooking for themselves. This kitchen provides every amenity a chef might need, accented with rustic elements like the counter's burled wood carvings. Opposite: Materials harvested from nature—wood floors, wool rugs, leather upholstery, and stone—create a great room with enduring style. Architect: Candace Tillotson-Miller, AIA, Miller Architects. Builder: Yellowstone Traditions.

Above: *The outdoorsperson's essentials, from walking sticks to fishing creels to hats, await the next expedition in this lodge-style home's hallway, lit by a moose horn chandelier and paved with stone flooring.*

Right: *Carved, cane-seated chairs flank the manor-size table in the dining area. The open kitchen's modern appliances are camouflaged by wood panels to fit right in to the lodge style.* **Opposite:** *Multipane windows and rough wood planking on the ceiling give this great room a feeling of age. Deep sofas and chairs welcome weary hunters back to a roaring fire after a day in the woods.*

MOD LODGE

THE LEGACY of the Adirondack Great Camps appears in today's lodge style, where fussy Victorian furnishings give way to pieces with simpler lines and larger sizes. This home also resembles its Old World ancestors—the baronial hunting lodges. Heavy tables and iron-strapped doors feel ancient and masculine. The beauty of wildlife is celebrated in animal and bird mounts, oil paintings, and antler chandeliers. And although the hunting lodges were built in the wilderness, they were by no means rough. Velvety fabrics, richly patterned tapestries, plush Oriental rugs, and warm lighting soften the lodge look. Bigger often means better when it comes to lodge style, so, here, the mass of the fireplace is accentuated by setting its stone chimney against a stacked stone wall. The home maintains a cozy feel, however, thanks in part to the lowered ceilings accented with hand-hewn beams in the kitchen and dining area.

WOODLAND FANTASY

OPENING THE HANDCRAFTED WOOD and etched-glass doors of this Midwestern home is like entering a gnome's hideaway in a hollow tree. The enchanted forest feel continues in the home's staircase, with its steps made of full-round logs and bordered with peeled log railings and balusters. In the living room, sections of a cedar tree trunk support the smooth cedar mantel. The home's classic lodge-style elements include king-post trusses in the living room, comfortable leather furnishings, deep-tinted log walls, and a sizable stone fireplace. An oversize plaid chair, arch-topped windows, and a grand piano are more traditional elements that blend smoothly with the rustic chinked log walls. The fire on the hearth, plush carpeting, and honey wood tones create an inviting space for all who enter this enchanted home.

Right: *Showstopping handmade doors pay tribute to the main ingredient of any log cabin: trees. In the entry, wood shines from the beams and truss overhead to the wide-planked floors underfoot.*

Left: *A beautiful rural setting is a central part of classic cabin style. These homeowners framed their landscape view with windows to bring the outdoors inside.* **Builder:** Town and Country Cedar Homes.

OLD WORLD ELEGANCE

IN THE DEEP SILENT CHILL of a winter's night, nothing is more inviting than a warm hunting lodge. This lodge-style home envelops visitors with languid warmth. Following in the tradition of Old World manors, the home's surfaces are richly patterned, from carved dining chairs covered in brocade to layered rugs and throw pillows to painted lampshades. The furnishings beckon with texture warm to the touch, while rich hues of red, green, and taupe create a cocoon of luxury. Metal and iron, twisted into ornate designs, form light fixtures that glow in soft pools of light. Logs appear here and there as accents in the home; for example, in simple ceiling trusses and as window trim.

Opposite: *Oversize furnishings, dark wood tones, and deeply colored walls underline the luxury of lodge style. Floral-patterned armchairs and bowls of fresh flowers add a hint of femininity to the room.* **Designer: Dolins Design Studio.**

Silk pillows, a floral duvet, and a mink throw soften this rustic log canopy bed, making it the perfect refuge on a long midwinter's night.

A round table with a wraparound view of the snowy woods sets the scene for elegant yet informal meals. Deep red walls and a wood-paneled ceiling warm the cool blue of the snowy landscape.

SMOOTHING OUT THE EDGES

WITH ITS ROOTS firmly planted in lodge style, this cabin has fun mixing a traditional look with contemporary updates. You can trace the home's style back to the Adirondack Great Camps and Old World retreats with their log walls and massive stone fireplaces. In this space, however, the logs are smaller in diameter and lighter in color. The fireplace, while still towering, is monochromatic and sculptural. And unlike the dark, closed-in hunting lodges of old, this home's vaulted ceilings soar, providing an open, airy feeling to the great room. The furnishings are simple in line but still luxurious. It's as if someone took the masculine lodge style and polished its rough edges until they were smooth. Still, you can imagine this home playing host to nature lovers and outdoorspeople with ease—such is the rugged appeal of logs in any setting.

Right: *In this bedroom, the patterned rug and folksy painted trunk contrast with the more contemporary fitted bedding and sleek Roman window shades.*

Above: *Even a large group could share an intimate meal in this cozy dining room. Rich window treatments and a medieval-inspired chandelier add pattern and color to the room.*

Opposite: *The great room's light fixture beautifully blends Western and Arts & Crafts styles. The whole room leads to the stunning mountain view framed by the window.* **Builder: Rocky Mountain Log Homes.**

A NATURAL BEAUTY

Opposite: *Masculine leather furniture is gathered around an Oriental rug that warms the stone-tiled floor of the great room. A wall of windows looks out over the home's wraparound deck.* **Builder:** **Montana Log Homes.**

IN AN UPDATED TAKE on the tradition of the Adirondack Great Camps, this home soars in architectural beauty yet remains down to earth and natural. Rustic logs that reveal their scars and fascinating imperfections are used as massive posts to support the vaulted ceiling. For the home's stairs, railings, beams, and handcrafted walls, skip-peeled logs are the natural choice to maintain the rustic feel. The Great Camp owners' love affair with twig furniture is rekindled here with twig tables and bent willow armchairs. What the Adirondack ancestors couldn't bring to their camps is this home's sweeping Rocky Mountain views and its luxurious outdoor whirlpool spa, among other modern-day amenities. Still, the log cabin surrounds itself with the trees of the forest, in good Great Camp style, and seems to have sprung naturally from the woods around it.

A graphic Navajo rug adds interest to the catwalk leading to the loft. The loft and its balcony give the feeling of living high in the treetops.

With its heavy overhangs and divided-pane windows, this log cabin echoes the storybook architecture of the Adirondack Great Camps. Bent willow chairs offer a spot to enjoy the mountain views.

Left: *By day, you may rough it in the great outdoors, but at night, this master bedroom offers luxurious comfort. A romantic fireplace and layers of downy bedding ensure sweet dreams.*

NEW BECOMES OLD AGAIN

A CHERISHED LOG CABIN glows with years of love and fond memories of time spent away from everyday cares. Even a new log cabin, like this one, can boast a well-loved feel. The key is to layer architectural features, furnishings, and accessories. This home's balcony, with its pole railings, recalls grand old lodges like the Old Faithful Inn in Yellowstone National Park. A heavy ceiling truss looks as old as a medieval cathedral. Hickory twig furniture takes its cue from rustic, north woods style, yet the home is spacious and comfortable enough to suit today's tastes. A key benefit of this layered decor is that it lends warmth to the home—warmth that feels as if it has accumulated over time.

An array of different looks fits under the umbrella of lodge style. In the entryway guarded by a carved Native American brave, an Arts & Crafts–style pendant light shines on a Southwestern-style bench and a collection of snowshoes.

Opposite: *A truly great room brings people together in one place for dining and living. Here, multiple seating areas allow guests to read in a plump chair by the fire or play cards at a round table.* Architect: Mark Deagle, The Jarvis Group Architects. Builder: Sun Forest Construction. Designer: Beth Slifer, Slifer Designs.

THE BEAUTY OF BIRCH

THE SILVERY BIRCH TREES of the upstate New York forests provided the Adirondack Great Camps with a versatile and beautiful building material. In this cabin, birch bark accented with twigs papers the gable walls and provides added interest to the fireplace. In the sitting area, whole birch logs with their bark intact frame another fireplace, while acting as support posts and beams for the ceiling. Smaller pieces of birch branches are fashioned into lamps, small tables, and baskets. To complement the white and gray of the birch bark, shades of deep red and blue are used throughout the home, in the cabin's upholstery, in its window treatments, and in the striking twig mosaic bed's spread and pillows. All together, the use of bark, twigs, branches, and logs give this cabin a sweet connection with the forest.

Above: *Twig mosaic accented with birch bark highlights this grand bed and night table. The room's narrow wood siding provides a vintage camp backdrop.*

Birch branches, with their papery bark, create interesting window trim and frame a distinctive settee in the corner of this sitting area. A wide picture window captures a view of the woods.

*An updated Adirondack style, stripped of
Victorian frill but instilled with comfort, gives
this living room a classic yet modern look.*

DESIGNED BY NATURE

Wᴴɪʟᴇ ᴛᴏᴅᴀʏ'ѕ ᴍᴀɴᴜꜰᴀᴄᴛᴜʀᴇʀѕ rely on machines and lathes to create fancy ornaments and turns on their mass-produced furniture, the rustic furniture makers of the Adirondack north woods used ingenuity and the abundance of the forest. From large case pieces to chairs to small boxes, the furniture and accessories created in rustic style all spotlight the beauty of nature. Craftspeople gathered twigs, bark, reeds, roots, and branches to use in their creations, and their patterns were gleaned from looks that were popular at the time, such as Victorian and Arts & Crafts styles. And although the heyday of the Adirondack Great Camps has passed, their influence is still seen in rustic furniture design. Like many of the pieces shown here, new furnishings and accessories are being made that honor the rustic tradition and its unique beauty.

A pattern of chip carvings dots the twigs on this gypsy chest. The piece's aged wood legs complement the piece's hickory top. **Manufacturer: Rustic Furniture.**

Pliable willow branches are harvested then bent into fanciful shapes to create unique twig furniture, such as this elaborate high-backed chair. **Manufacturer: Sleeping Bear Twig Furniture.**

Bright red chairs would add zest to any cabin's breakfast nook or great room. This table and chair set gives a nod to the classic shade of red favored by the owners of the Great Camps. **Manufacturer: Whispering Pines.**

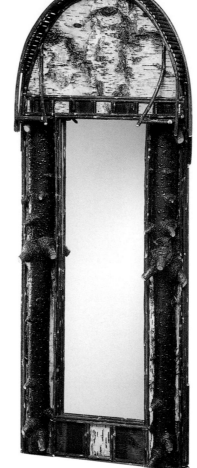

This simple arched mirror reveals the beauty of bark, featuring both the reddish hues from the inner layers of birch bark and the outer layer's peachy shade of white. Manufacturer: Sleeping Bear Twig Furniture.

A tufted lounger with the look of a classic leather armchair would add straightforward masculinity to any lodge-style cabin. Manufacturer: Hancock & Moore.

Four shed antlers balance on a moose horn, which serves as the base for this floor lamp. Even the lamp's finial is a section of antler. Manufacturer: Antler Artistry.

Trompe l'oeil painting gives a fly-fishing theme to this cheerful coffee table. The table's legs and twig accents follow in the rustic furniture tradition. Manufacturer: Whispering Pines.

THE WILD WEST

WE LOVE TO HEAR the story of how the West was won. Movies, TV shows, and Western novels tell tall tales of cowboy heroes and their faithful sidekicks over and over again. And when he's not sleeping under the stars, we just know the cowboy goes home to a log cabin. Bringing Western style to a log cabin means seeing beauty in everyday objects—a hand-tooled saddle, woven blankets, and the simple forms of Native American pottery. No fluff and nonsense here, Missy; just plain and simple folks doing their jobs and living their lives. Western style is honest, practical, and sturdy—perfect for log cabins. Because the style is hardworking, the furnishings are rugged, like leather upholstered chairs and sturdy plank tables, and the colors are natural. Of course, a love of Cowboys and Indians can be taken to the extreme. The Technicolor Western style of Hollywood matinees and Route 66 souvenir stands can bring whimsy and fun to any plainspoken Western-style home.

Left: *This home where the buffalo roam showcases the best of Western style and artistry, from Molesworth furnishings made with burled wood to Native American beaded drapes.* **Manufacturer: New West. Above:** *Red leather and brass tacks spark interest in this sideboard, complete with wood inlay and branchy drawer pulls.* **Manufacturer: Viers Furniture Co.**

HOME, HOME ON THE RANGE

A WORKING RANCH is a no-frills kind of place. You come inside when night falls and get up with the sun. Besides a bed, all you need from the house is a place to grab some grub and wash off the trail dust. This log cabin is a chip off the ol' ranch house block, but it still creates a place comfy enough to settle in and put your boots up. Hand-peeled logs lined with white chinking create the backdrop for low-key style. Rustic furniture and a nothing-fancy decor make a home that's perfect for relaxing, but one that will still stand up to the rough and tumble. This isn't the place for brand-spanking-new things. The surfaces are matte or textured, like the stone on the fireplace and the split logs that line the kitchen's peninsula.

Above: *The whole crew can wash up at this trough-style sink in the bathroom. The sink is set into a countertop made from hand-hewn timber.*

Left: *When the dinner bell rings, folks head straight to this rustic kitchen, complete with a wood-topped peninsula. A round log beam defines the kitchen area in the high-ceilinged room.*

Opposite: *To maintain the rustic feel of this space, modern gadgets like televisions, VCRs, and stereos are hidden away in cabinets on either side of the living room's fireplace. The homestead is spruced up a bit with flowers and candles and such, but it would still feel just right to the ranch hands.* Architect: Candace Tillotson-Miller, AIA, Miller Architects. Designer: Gandy Peace, Inc.

COWBOY HIGH STYLE

EASTERNERS WHO HEADED WEST in the early 1900s looking for adventure made themselves at home in dude ranches. These ranches were gussied-up versions of the real thing, filled with high-style furnishings that celebrated the myth of the Cowboys-and-Indians past. Thomas Molesworth, a Cody, Wyoming, furniture maker, started the trend with his contemporary furniture upholstered with leather in primary colors or Chimayo weavings and emblazoned with symbols of the Old West. He also incorporated burled wood into his furniture for added interest and peeled logs and branches for an organic appeal. This home follows in the spirit of those early dude ranches, with its flamboyant Western accents—from buckskin drapes to Navajo rugs to pony-skin throw pillows. Tiffany-style lamps recall the Victorian decor brought to the West by pioneering Easterners.

Opposite: *As comfortable as a pair of broken-in boots, leather chairs and a matching sofa gather 'round the living room's fireplace. Antler sconces and mounted animal trophies give a nod to the wildlife of the West.* **Builder: Montana Log Homes.**

Above: *A wagon wheel bench brings the Western style right outside. Like the cabins of early settlers, this home is built of round logs stacked atop each other and locked together with carved saddle-notch corners.*

Left: *Window treatments and upholstery take up the Western theme in the dining room, including these Molesworth-inspired chairs covered in pony skin and the burl table. Heavy Native American blankets add a dose of color to the windows and complement the Navajo rug below.*

Left: *Another beautiful fireplace charms the dining area. Here, massive Spanish-style chairs are grouped around a heavy wood table beneath an ornate chandelier. The flexibility of adobe allows for niches to be built into the walls to display artwork and sacred objects.*

ABSOLUTELY ADOBE

FOR MANY CENTURIES, the peoples of the Southwest have known how to build houses out of nothing but earth. From clay blocks called adobe, they build artfully sculpted homes that shelter them from the desert heat. Oftentimes, trees are used to support the ceiling structure. Logs, called *vigas,* span the distance between walls and are topped with smaller branches, called *latillas,* which, in turn, are topped with adobe. This home follows in the tradition of adobe houses and shows another cabin style— Southwestern. This style carries the influence of several groups of people: the Native Americans who lived in the region, the Spanish and Mexicans who colonized the area, and the Easterners who ventured to the Southwest in search of land. The climate of the Southwest and its natural resources also influence the style.

All of the raw materials of Southwestern style are here: curving adobe walls, hand-forged metal, saltillo tiles, and stout log posts. The high arches echo the shape of the beehive fireplace and recall the architecture of Spanish missions.

Opposite: *The warmth of wood in the ceiling and window trim accents the soft white walls of adobe in this great room. The multifaced fireplace commands attention in the center of the room. Architect: Otwell Architects. Designer: Dorado Designs, Inc. Interior designer: Mary Margaret Interior Design.*

LIVING THE LEGEND

IMAGINE THE EASTERNERS who booked a stay at the Western dude ranches of the early 1900s. They crossed the country by railroad, eager to arrive at a Rocky Mountain ranch where they could try their hands at riding and roping and get a taste of the cowboy life. These vacationing dudes expected to find the romance of the Old West—along with all the comforts of home—in their bunkhouses. This small ranch cabin fits the bill. Molesworth-style leather furniture, a warm fireplace, and a well-stocked bar keep visitors content. The log cabin's low ceilings, lined with plywood and accented with simple square beams, make the place intimate and cozy. In a pine-paneled bedroom, a cloud-shape bed lulls dudes to sleep after hours spent riding the range. The buffalo robe above the headboard and the matching bedside lamps carry out the Old West feel.

Opposite: Classic dude ranch decor prevails in this cabin. A Navajo rug on the floor and a rawhide-and-iron light fixture overhead set the scene.

Above: *Quarter-round pieces of wood were sometimes used instead of chinking to fill the gaps between logs and to make a cabin's walls more weather tight. The dresser, with its antler drawer pulls, repeats the round face of the logs.*

Left: *When buffalo roamed, a hunt could yield buffalo robes like the one hung above this bed. Native Americans traditionally tanned and then painted the hides with bold patterns or figures.*

Right: By the sculptural adobe fireplace, bronze statues immortalize the horse and rider. Simple, rustic furnishings and rugged leather upholstery recall the hardworking past of Southwestern ranches.

Much of what indigenous peoples made by hand out of necessity has now become viewed as art. Here, Navajo weavings are prized for their graphic beauty, and handmade leather saddles are displayed as artwork along the balcony.

SOUTHWEST RANCH DRESSING

RANCHING brought another influence on traditional Southwestern style. The simple ranch house and the culture surrounding horses and cowboys add a graphic element to the style. This ranch house offers simple construction: adobe walls, ceilings accented by log *vigas,* and wide-planked wood floors. Its unique style comes from the tools of the trade displayed throughout the home, from saddles and tack to cowboy hats and handwoven saddle blankets. Fireplaces, typically tucked into a corner, hurry off the evening chill, while Navajo rugs warm the floors. The kitchen is designed to fit the needs of a chef but is durable enough to stand up to a pack of ranch hands hungry for a meal. Muted colors inside reflect the subtle palette of the Southwest land. And comfortable, simple furnishings invite weary ranchers to come in and sit a spell.

Opposite: A trio of hand-forged iron rods holds the ranch's collection of copper pots and pans, perfect for rustling up some grub. Simple cabinets are topped with long-wearing granite and wood countertops.

NATURAL WONDERS

WESTERN STYLE can be as big as the mountains and plains outside. This home springs from the vast, unspoiled West and focuses on its first residents—the Native Americans. Rugs, blankets, pottery, and baskets crafted by skilled Native American artisans set the color palette for the earthy browns, tans, and reds of the home's decor. A drum topped with taut cowhide serves as a unique table. Like the indigenous peoples, these homeowners used the materials of nature to create their home. River rock is stacked into a chimney and massive walls. Logs form the stairs, posts, beams, fireplace mantels, and walls. Flat stones serve as flooring, and leather and wool upholster the furniture. The home's windows thoughtfully frame the valley and mountain views, making the outdoors a central part of the overall look.

Opposite: *A soaring great room offers plenty of space for multiple seating areas, including one around the fire's warmth and another that basks in the panoramic views.* **Architect: Jerry Locati.**

Wide windows, undivided by panes, push this seating area out into the sunlit trees. Neutral upholstery allows the view to take center stage.

Towering chandeliers are fashioned from antlers. Animals shed their antlers each year, leaving behind in the forest the raw material for these classic Western light fixtures.

Left: *Ready for a cowboy's Saturday evening bath, this shiny red tub is the focal point for the master bath area. Contemporary glass block lends privacy to the shower area.*

Log cabin style should be inviting. A welcoming archway and a bench to sit on while you pull off your boots make folks feel right at home.

EAST COAST COWBOY

WHEN A HOME welcomes you with a "Howdy!" plaque hung over the entry, you know its owners like a bit of whimsy in their home's interior design. This log home, located in the Southeast, adds a generous helping of humor to its unique blend of Western and Southwestern decor. Bright colors, folksy artwork, and a willingness to mix styles make this home both lively and comfortable. Vibrant color pops up in the kitchen's painted cabinetry, on woven Navajo rugs, in denim upholstery, and even in the master bath's showstopping red tub. The logs that back up the style are rounded and finished in a light honey tone that's complemented by the rich wood flooring. The informal, open floor plan, with a loft overlooking the kitchen and great room below, underscores the home's warm welcome.

Opposite: *Mexican* saltillo *tiles line the kitchen's backsplash, while colorful stained glass pendant lights shine on the casual breakfast bar. The bar stools, made of bleached wood, carry out the Southwestern motif.* **Builder: Rocky Mountain Log Homes.**

Chrome yellow chairs bring electric warmth to the dining area, which is lit by a bleached antler chandelier. The table is set with a collection of handmade pottery.

WESTERN SOPHISTICATE

CABIN STYLE fits connoisseurs, too. This Colorado log home is filled with Molesworth-inspired furniture and a museum-quality collection of Western and Native American artifacts. Every detail is looked after, from the rows of brass tacks on the sofas' upholstery to the beaded and fringed white cowhide drapes that hang from iron spears. Although it's a showpiece, the home still offers great comfort. Window seats provide a perch to drink in the view. Warm woven upholstery and luxurious colors encourage long visits. The central, two-sided fireplace displays the owner's outdoorsy interests while warming both the living area and the dining room. The homeowner's fascination with the past shows in his collection of Native American arrowheads; the coffee table fashioned from ancient, petrified wood; and the flooring made of wood salvaged from a 19th-century mill.

Opposite: *While the black leather and burled wood sofas resemble the furnishings crafted by Thomas Molesworth for early 1900's dude ranches, they are actually custom-made contemporary pieces. The hearth features a mantel fashioned out of round logs that complement the lodgepole pine used throughout the home and provide a perfect perch for snowshoes and other outdoorsy elements.* **Manufacturer: New West. Styling: Debra Grahl.**

FILLED WITH FLAVOR

A RANCH HOUSE should offer comfort and function. This home does just that—and makes it all look good. Using every inch of space, this log cabin ranch includes an open kitchen, a dining area surrounded by windows, and a cozy living room warmed by a stone fireplace. The kitchen's rough-sided cabinets are painted a sage green, setting them off from the rest of the room and adding a splash of color. In classic log cabin style, a sleeping loft overlooks the living room, which features a carefully edited selection of ranch elements. The home's squared logs are accented with white chinking; above, square beams support the loft and help define the kitchen and dining area. The floor is lined with rugged wood planks to stand up to the daily stampede of boots and spurs.

Above: *An antler chandelier and burnished leather chairs hint at classic ranch decor, while the open kitchen provides modern amenities in a rustic setting.*

Right: *In a smaller cabin, paring down accessories can keep the room open. Here, a steer head is centered above the mantel and flanked by simple candlesticks and a ceramic pot.*

Opposite: *A quartet of red throw pillows accents the hickory settee's kilim upholstery. The red color is repeated in the loft bed's quilt.* Architect: Richard Dooley. Builder: Custom Log Homes.

WONDER OF THE WEST

THE GAMES of Cowboys and Indians that some kids like to play revolve around the myths of warriors and weapons. This home celebrates not the warfare of the Old West but the artistry. The native and pioneer artisans who hand-tooled leather, beaded hats and clothing, wove blankets and rugs, and made furniture by hand are the heroes of this Western home. Like an old legend told around a campfire, this home is larger than life in its collections and tributes to the characters who won the West. A ground-floor media room resembles a cave, complete with ancient petroglyphs. The room's cool stone steps become comfy seating places thanks to a colorful array of pillows and throws. A hallway-turned-gallery displays a lifetime collection of Western wear and cowboy hats. The collection continues in the sitting room, where a love seat swims in waves of woven pillows and throws.

Right: *The ordinary act of watching a film is made extraordinary in this cavelike media room. Cushioned sofas with flocks of throw pillows covered in Native and South American weavings soften the stone surroundings.*

Above: *The backdrop for this collection of Western gear is rustic and antiquated. Overhead, logs form simple archways, while wide stone pavers line the floor below. Even the hardware on the doors recalls the Old West.*

Right: *Beneath a swooping ceiling that gives the feel of a tent, a rustic Southwestern chest is the center of attention in a sitting area piled high with Native American blankets, weavings, and rugs.*

SIMPLY WESTERN

SOUTHWESTERN-, ranch-, and Western-style homes are structurally simple. No fancy architecture is required to create a backdrop for these looks. Natural and authentic materials used in simple ways will make your cabin's Western decor ring true. But the right furnishings, accessories, and finishes are essential in order to nail the look. You can't go wrong with oversize furnishings upholstered in natural-colored leather. Navajo rugs on the floor underline the style, and collections that interest you—from Native American pottery to cowboy boots—will give your cabin that Western twang. Don't overlook your home's light fixtures. From antler chandeliers to kitschy chuck-wagon table lamps, searching for the perfect lighting will lead you to wonderful and whimsical sources.

Made at the turn of the 20th century, this Native American coiled basket depicts a striking graphic pattern in black and white. **Manufacturer: Natalie Fay Linn Native American Baskets.**

A Native American basket shape blooms in iron in this table lamp. The lampshade is painted by hand and accented with a pattern of leather lacings. **Manufacturer: Cloudbird.**

An octagonal game table set on a giant wood burl offers plenty of elbow room for poker games. Carved keyhole chairs complete the set. **Manufacturer: Santos Furniture.**

A heavily burled Molesworth-style arm- chair and matching ottoman are upholstered in leather and Chimayo weavings. **Manufacturer: Viers Furniture Co.**

Above: *A Native American cabinet depicts the rough and tumble of life on the Western frontier. Carved Indian heads accent the Southwestern-style piece.* **Manufacturer: Livingston Furniture Design.**

Carved coyotes flank a buffalo head on this love seat's frame, while wildlife silhouettes appear on its accent pillows. **Manufacturer: Santos Furniture.**

THE SUMMER PLACE

O N THE FIRST DAY of summer camp, you checked into your cabin and found bunk beds, wood floors, and log walls carved with campers' initials. Some of your best childhood memories may have been created there. Camp and cottage styles remind us of summer's halcyon days—but without the bug spray and flashlights. If your idea of paradise is a getaway in the woods, your style might include Pendleton blankets and bearskin rugs. If your vacation idyll is near the water, your cottage might take a nautical turn, with whitewashed plank paneling and a hammock on the porch. Camp and cottage styles make room for the vintage rocker and faded florals cast off from Grandma's city house as well as Grandpa's creels, fishing poles, and canoe paddles. The furnishings and accessories in a summer place should be just one step removed from the outdoors. In fact, many of them may be used both inside and out—the table that's carried to the porch for supper and the quilt that's spread out on the lawn to watch Fourth of July fireworks are the stuff of cottage and summer camp styles.

Left: *Casual wicker is the perfect furniture for cottage looks. This armchair in a rich mahogany shade pulls close to the fire for reading in the evening.* **Above:** *A log cabin isn't just for summer. This snowshoe lamp recalls the crisp days of winter, when being snowed in equals the ideal romantic getaway.* Manufacturer: Whispering Pines.

GOING OUT ON A WHIM

THE INTERIOR DESIGN of a summer camp isn't planned so much as it is accumulated. For example, a new kitchen table at home means the old one gets carted off to camp. China and silverware follow the same route. At camp, almost anything goes: An antique clock and a minnow bucket both belong on the mantel. If you need to hang up your fishing rods, you just screw a pair of hooks into the living room wall. Well-worn quilts cover the beds and, on occasion, are dragged outside for a picnic by the lake. The kitchen is simple, open, and used by everyone for washing berries, fixing supper, or cleaning fish. In this hunting and fishing cabin, the space is tied together by logs accented in shades of green—a perfect fit for these woodsy surroundings. Even the refrigerator gets a lift from a campy makeover.

Above: *In this bedroom and throughout the cabin, interior shutters can be lowered and latched when it's time to leave camp. The window's divided panes are reminiscent of cabins from years past.*

Left: *If rainy weather sets in, a table for card playing and plenty of easy chairs for reading help ward off cases of cabin fever. A braided rug underfoot complements the unique red, white, and green plaid refrigerator.* **Opposite:** *A collection of stools provides put-your-feet-up comfort in the living room. A fireplace or woodstove is a camp essential. Where else would you gather for ghost stories and s'mores?* **Designer: Pump & Circumstance.**

Left: *The log walls are on display in the kitchen, instead of being covered up by cabinets hung on the walls. Open shelves are supported by curved branches.*

A white cotton bedspread lends a crisp touch to the bedroom's mix of floral patterns. Just outside the French doors, a private balcony looks out over the lake.

NORTH WOODS GETAWAY

TIME MOVES IN SLOW MOTION at a summer cottage. Many a long afternoon is spent just walking a dirt road and picking wildflowers for a simple bouquet. The evening twilight stretches out with enough space for rowdy games of dominoes or quiet time reading a favorite novel. Dinners become drawn-out feasts of fresh vegetables and cookouts flavored with fresh air. In the morning, you wake to the sunshine— not an alarm clock. In this log cabin home, quaint divided-pane windows open wide to breezes off the lake. Cheery red cabinets in the kitchen make putting together picnics even more fun. And French doors in the bedroom open to bring the sounds of the forest and the lake's gentle lapping inside.

Left: *Touches of red make this intimate living room even more cozy. The window trim is painted evergreen, a classic north woods cottage color.* **Builder: Alpine Log Homes, Inc.**

Right: *Snowshoes, a pheasant trophy, and a campy coffee kettle are reminders of the north woods camp tradition. The open floor plan allows the woodstove's heat to rise and warm the loft area.*

Above: *Log beams and walls make this bedroom cozy and quiet. Camp bedrooms offer simple amenities—a chest of drawers for storage, a lamp to read by, and a warm quilt for cool nights.*

OPEN SEASON

AS SURE AS mosquitoes rise from a swamp, a log cabin camp attracts visitors. Here, a new camp offers plenty of space for both family and friends. If you're outfitting a summer place, start with a long camp table and plenty of chairs. Add comfortable sofas and a generous sleeping loft, and soon your camp will be ready for company. Remember to make the kitchen large enough for guests to pitch in with the dishes, and plan a master bedroom tucked away from the crowd. This home's cozy style radiates from the cast-iron woodstove. Classic Windsor dining chairs complement the look and provide comfortable seats for even the longest late-night card games. Plaid upholstery on the sofas hides stains well, so you can relax when guests show up with their kids and pets in tow.

Opposite: *A log-trimmed catwalk spans the great room and leads to a second-floor balcony over the front porch. The home's logs are skip-peeled to give them a mottled pattern.* **Builder: Lok-N-Logs.**

Above: *Grab your rod, reel, and net— the fish are really biting! A handpainted bench captures the sunny exuberance of summer vacation. Simple tile floors make cleaning the cabin a snap.*

ARTISTIC LICENSE

WHEN THERE'S AN ARTIST in residence, especially one who imparts everything around her with joy, color will bubble up to the surface. This cottage-style log cabin in the northern Midwest almost giggles with the fun of summer. Scraps of fabrics and button collections play on pillows, and daubs of paint decorate chairs, benches, and framed artwork with a riot of images. And even though the cabin is filled with fun, it takes comfort seriously. Deep armchairs and a stone fireplace make the living room a wonderful place to gather in the evening. Soft coverlets layer the beds and provide a nice contrast to the rustic frame made of tree branches. Broad screened porches offer the fragrance of night air, without pesky mosquitoes. The stage is set for a magical week at the lake, no matter if the fish are biting or not.

Right: *Vintage textiles hanging at the window and piled on the bed charm the cabin's bedroom. The bed and curtain rod showcase the appealing natural curves of tree branches.* **Opposite:** *The casual side of cottage style appears in the living room. Colors and prints mix and match into a joyful jumble that somehow all works together.*

SWEET DREAMS, CAMPERS

I T JUST WOULDN'T BE summer camp without a bunk room full of kids whispering knock-knock jokes and playing flashlight tag. The treelike bunk beds pictured here are fashioned from branches to give lucky campers the sense of sleeping out in the woods—without the fear of wayward bears. Each set of beds offers a simple ladder to reach the much-coveted top bunk and is topped off with warm and colorful camp blankets or denim duvets to add style and warmth. The decor of a bunk room should be simple. All that's needed is a place to bed down and lots of storage space for gear. Wood paneling or logs make the rooms' walls indestructible—perfect for enduring pillow fights and bouts of wrestling. As an added touch, a few Western accessories and an assortment of Navajo rugs are scattered throughout to spark a child's fantasy of the cowboy life.

Above: *A simple ladder-style log bunk bed makes room for two tired cow-pokes. A lasso, cowboy boots, and framed Western movie posters add to the fun.* Builder: Montana Log Homes.

Right: *After a long day on the slopes, this pair of unique bunk beds offers comfort. A whole slumber party can curl up in this bunk room, tucked beneath a log home's rafters.* Builder: Rocky Mountain Log Homes.

Six sleepy campers can catch some winks in this space-saving bunk room. Windows and a ceiling fan allow for cool breezes on summer nights. Architect: Candace Tillotson-Miller, AIA, Miller Architects. Designer: Gandy Peace, Inc.

PRINTS CHARMING

Just as an English country garden bursts with life and color, a cottage-style home charms its owners with cheery colors and surrounds them with comfort. Cottage style is softly extravagant in its layering of print and pattern, creating a look that's both fresh and gently lived-in. The warmth of wood looks as at home in this style as trees do in a garden. In this log cabin, wood appears in heavy posts as trim for windows and doors, in the polished stair railings, and in the dark hued floor of the great room. From a whimsical bedroom draped in canvas to resemble a tent to one decked out in plaids, ticking stripes, and floral prints, this home creates a welcoming, even romantic, getaway from high-tech life.

Above: *Drapes as sheer as a summer chemise enclose the head of this well-dressed bed. Crisp stripes tailor the ruffled downy chair.*

Left: *This indoor tent celebrates the passions of outdoorspeople, from boaters to hikers to campers. A kayak becomes a piece of sculpture hung from the ceiling. Its bright red is echoed in the bed's Hudson's Bay point blanket.* **Opposite:** *Leather club chairs and a game table bring a masculine touch to the great room, while shades of green and rose warm the sofas.*

CHERISHED MEMORIES

THOSE LUCKY ENOUGH to own a summer camp or cottage return there year after year, accumulating memories that are echoed in the cabin's accessories. At the cottage, the humble is seen as beautiful, the whimsical is beloved, and the items that have seen better days are cherished. Rocks a toddler gathered on a walk through the woods are displayed like artwork. A dented enamel pitcher once used for lemonade now holds bunches of wildflowers. Children are tucked in for the night beneath snowy chenille bedspreads. In the summer camp, silly signs and kitschy souvenirs find a place next to the abundance of outdoor gear, like fishing poles, canoe paddles, horseshoes, and more. Comfort is key to this cabin style, which welcomes all to come as they are.

Above: *A spruce green Adirondack chair like this one is the quintessential chair of summer, whether it's perched at the end of a dock for sunbathing or stationed on the lawn for watching Fourth of July fireworks.* **Manufacturer: Whispering Pines. Right:** *Cabin style, especially in a summer camp, is warm and inviting. These folksy felt pillows reinforce that welcoming feeling.* **Manufacturer: Whispering Pines.**

What's a summer spent at a camp without a few wildlife sightings? These bear bookends will add whimsy to any cabin bookshelf. **Manufacturer: Whispering Pines.**

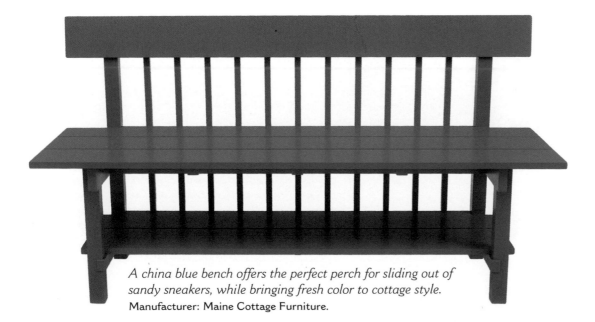

To light the walls of a summer camp, a school of rainbow trout swims along this sconce crafted in steel. **Manufacturer: Avalanche Ranch Light Company.**

A china blue bench offers the perfect perch for sliding out of sandy sneakers, while bringing fresh color to cottage style. **Manufacturer: Maine Cottage Furniture.**

A traditional wood-topped wicker table is given a shot of celadon green to capture the color of a tulip leaf as it bursts to the surface. **Manufacturer: Maine Cottage Furniture.**

In a warm shade of ivory that would go well with any decor, this sideboard and hutch recall time spent at Grandma's cottage on the lake. **Manufacturer: Maine Cottage Furniture.**

Beadboard, with its pattern of vertical grooves, echoes the wainscoting and kitchen cabinets found in many vintage cottages. **Manufacturer: Maine Cottage Furniture.**

Bear, moose, deer, and elk circle this wildlife chandelier. The metal's rust patina glows with light softened by kraft paper lamp shades. **Manufacturer: Avalanche Ranch Light Company.**

TODAY'S LOG LOOKS

IN THE 1930S, plywood, a product manufactured of wood veneer, was first put to use to build a home's structure. Midcentury modernists eagerly incorporated plywood's fresh face into home decor. And while these forward-thinkers probably considered log homes hopelessly old-fashioned, their style does fit with logs. The key is to keep things light. Whitewashed wood walls, large windows, and pale floors set the scene for contemporary design. The rounded rhythm of log walls makes an intriguing foil for the pared-down geometric shapes of contemporary furniture and accessories. One place where modern looks especially at home is the kitchen. With today's stainless-steel appliances and variety of stone and cement countertops, the contemporary kitchen is winning fans with all kinds of tastes. In the kitchen and throughout the contemporary home, logs can add a hint of warmth to what can seem austere. Metals, particularly those with matte finishes, also go well with logs. In stair railings, faucets, and light fixtures, metal cools the logs' warmth and adds contemporary flair. The wide-open spaces of today's log homes, especially their vaulted ceilings, create expanses for hanging modern artwork or installing banks of windows.

Left: *This great room offers a blend of styles, from Old World furnishings and twiggy railings to more modern touches like the glass coffee table and contemporary table lamps.* Builder: Maple Island Log Homes. **Above:** *From its flirty curlicued base to its leafy finial, this highland candlestick lamp mixes styles with flair and tops it off with a slim rawhide shade.* Manufacturer: Cloudbird.

Wood cabinetry and richly hued flooring warms the kitchen's cool blue wall and stainless-steel countertops. Overhead, metal mesh is set with recessed lights.

To add a modern touch to any cabin, choose a staircase with an industrial feel. Here, black metal risers and cables are topped with a blond wood handrail.

COLOR IT CONTEMPORARY

CABIN STYLE can include modern looks, especially those punctuated with color and created with a desire for warmth and livability. Blond wood forms the warm but understated backdrop for this contemporary home. A cobalt blue wall divides the space and frames the sleek kitchen. To contrast the cool blue, the kitchen is awash in rusty red, including the stained concrete below—a trendy yet informal choice for flooring that's perfect for log homes. Clever wrought-iron sconces are affixed to the kitchen wall's red posts to provide a glow to the space. This same lighting treatment is repeated in the vaulted open space to accent the thin black metal rods and cables used instead of traditional log trusses. Leather chairs and simple slip-covered sofas gather into a warm nest in the living area. The entire look is polished but warm.

An open floor plan—a popular choice among log cabin owners—allows guests in the living room and dining area to enjoy the fireplace. **Architect: Stephen Dynia Architects.**

Left: *Open kitchens are a relatively new invention in American homes. Their informality is perfect for cabin style, where guests can step right in and help the cook—or at least pull up a chair and feel part of the action.*

Above: *Heavy logs call for furnishings with weight. This chunky console table complements the heavy frame on the mirror. A pair of antlers recalls the home's north woods relatives.*

OVERARCHING COMFORT

Opposite: *Archways add grace and curvy appeal to any home. This arch reveals the true mass of the wall logs. A second archway beyond leads into the kitchen.* **Builder: Montana Log Homes.**

WHILE PEOPLE once purchased furniture in matched sets, today's homeowners are more likely to mix than match their furnishings. The eclectic style of decorating, which incorporates pieces of various vintages and wide-ranging looks, gives you the opportunity to make your cabin's decor uniquely yours. This home pulls from the Western tradition of building with large round logs accented with chinking and brings in elements from a variety of other styles. For example, the armchairs that flank the fireplace can be traced back to Colonial wing chairs. The kitchen's compact woodstove follows a north woods tradition, while the cabinets have simple, almost Shaker-style faces. Above, modern black track lights provide task lighting for the kitchen's work areas. Together, these pieces create a comfortable family home with a distinct personality.

TAKING LOGS TO NEW HEIGHTS

ECLECTIC STYLE encompasses the grand as well as the cozy, as displayed in this log cabin. The key to the home's unique style is that it balances awe-inspiring architecture with warmth and livability. Handcrafted logs add the necessary warmth, while the interior decor brings color and comfort. The vaulted great room comprises the living room, dining area, and kitchen, but each room has its own elegant identity that complements its neighbors. For example, the bar in the kitchen is mirrored by a low wall that defines the dining area. Wood flooring and the log posts and beams tie the whole room together. The kitchen's stone walls are repeated in the master bedroom, where round log beams give way to ornate timber-framed trusses.

Opposite: *Quietly elegant armchairs and leather sofas civilize the massive logs used for the home's structure. Navajo patterned rugs and a bronze wildlife sculpture give a nod to the Western mountain location.* Architect: Strout Architects. Builder: High Country Log Homes. Designer: Anna Peavy.

Left: *An armoire painted with a mountain land-scape fits right in to this larger-than-life bedroom. A simple log bed is layered with vibrant color to contrast the room's stone walls.*

LET THERE BE LIGHT

BRINGING THE OUTDOORS INSIDE is a benefit to any log home, whether the decorating scheme is Arts & Crafts, Southwestern, cottage, or casual eclectic, as in this home. While you may not be able to have a great room with a wall full of windows, you can achieve a similar effect with rustic wood furnishings, stone accents, and floral textiles. Continuing its nod to nature, this cabin's massive stone fireplace is only outdone by the unique twiggy loft railings, which are a modern take on the twig and branch elements made popular by the Great Camps. The blend of styles doesn't stop here, though. An Arts & Crafts–style floor lamp sheds light on a leather chair that looks like it was taken straight out of an Old World hunting lodge. The chair's matching sofas fit right in next to a pair of Victorian-style armchairs. The mix-and-match look continues in the loft area, where a campy bear statue watches over the space.

Above: *The home's loft is made unique by its railings made of curvy twigs and branches. Skylights accent the high ceilings and shed more light on the space.*

Right: *Curvy branches come together to form an amazing bedstead, with a wooden perch at the end of the bed for putting on shoes and socks. The sliding glass door and windows echo the style in the great room.*

Opposite: *Great doesn't even begin to describe the windows towering over this great room. Comfy leather furnishings provide the perfect place to take in the stunning view.* **Builder: Maple Island Log Homes.**

COOL AND CONTEMPORARY

WESTERN LOGS add warmth to this Eastern contemporary home, which features streamlined furniture, black iron railings, and cool shades of stony gray to give the space a modern edge. Splashes of color in the rugs, upholstery, and accessories add a needed spark. To bring contemporary style to your cabin, look for simple lines, and eliminate anything fussy or frilly. Bold geometric shapes, like this home's blocky fireplace, squared floor tiles, and rectilinear iron bed, underscore the modern look. The vaulted ceilings, painted white and accented with log beams, give a refreshing airiness. Although the logs are bleached to cool their naturally warm tones, rich wood accents that radiate warmth can be found throughout the space, specifically in the dining room floor and furniture. The bedroom's cool sophistication comes from fitted bedclothes and linens in various shades of neutral.

Above: *Tiny halogen reading lamps accessorize this sleek bedroom. A backdrop of white bead board sets the bed out away from the log wall and makes it even more striking.*

Right: *This home's modernistic tendencies show in its linear iron stair railings and graphic wood and stone floor treatment. Cowhide shades soften the light from an iron chandelier.*

Opposite: *In the living room, a Stickley-style armchair upholstered in red gets along just fine with the clean-lined sofas and a blocky stone coffee table.* **Architect: Michael Ryan Architects. Builder: Alpine Log Homes, Inc.**

A WOODSY RETREAT

W HEN THE GREAT OUTDOORS is the main attraction, all you need from a log cabin is running water, a stove, and a place to sleep. Of course, time spent at the cabin is that much more enjoyable if the place is comfortable and pretty. This home fulfills all those needs and more. Classic log cabin styling contributes a stone fireplace, round log ceiling trusses, window seats, and a sleeping loft. Careful attention to comfort provides a getaway with generous seating, warm wood floors, and layers of pillows and throws. The cabin's good looks come from the owner's willingness to mix styles: Native American designs can be found in artwork and on pillows and throws, country plaids upholster the seating around the fire, and masculine stripes and paisleys cover the bedroom in layers of comfort. Of course, part of the home's beauty is its picture-perfect views of the shimmering stand of white birches and green leafy trees of summer.

Above: *A sunny, well-cushioned window seat becomes a personal retreat in this bedroom. Stout antique furnishings complement the mass of the tall log walls.*

Opposite: *Antique accessories, including an assortment of table lamps, add to this living room's country charm. The arched fireplace and stuffed deer mount are classic north woods elements.* **Builder: Alpine Log Homes, Inc. Right:** *A pole ladder leads to the sleeping loft over the kitchen. The long bench in front of the bar is the perfect perch for informal meals or chatting with the cook.*

ALL AGLOW

A GUEST HOUSE adjacent to a Western ski resort home reveals modern style in a warm, woodsy setting. The house is oriented around a three-sided stone fireplace that makes for a natural gathering spot. Plywood and planed wood beams create the backdrop for the clean-lined contemporary furniture, some of which was designed by the home's architect. The sofas' cobalt blue is echoed in the pool table and provides a jolt of color in the great room. In the kitchen, black countertops contrast smoothly with the shiny stainless-steel appliances. The space glows with warmth in the evening, but guests are still lured outside to the home's roof-top deck, where they can drink in a stunning view of the slopes and relax in the hot tub.

Above right: *The honey tones of the wood infuse this dining room with inviting warmth. A distinctive glass table and slatted wood chairs echo the clean-lined symmetry of the wine cellar beyond.*
Right: *A lowered ceiling lit by pendant lamps defines the sleek and elegant kitchen area. Wide, horizontal windows frame the mountain view.*

Left: *Featuring a floor plan that's contemporary, relaxed, and open, this guest house offers plenty of space for families to spend time together off the slopes. The three-sided fireplace is a stunning focal point that draws guests in from all corners of the space.* **Architect: Mark Pynn, AIA, McMillen Pynn Architecture LLP.**

How lovely it would be to wake up in this sweet sleeping alcove, with its sunburst pediment. The space offers a view of the trees and both a measure of privacy and access to the sitting area.

From the rich honey tones of the main house, a vaulted walkway leads to the guest quarters. Crisp white walls and a patterned floor hint at the decor of the adjacent rooms.

A diminutive seating area, complete with a charming fireplace, is tucked beneath the eaves of this guest house. Wide windows open the space to the wooded view.
Builder: Maple Island Log Homes.

SWEETNESS AND LIGHT

Part of the fun of decorating a cabin is introducing an element of the unexpected. This guest house throws the image of log cabins as dark and cramped right out the window. Whitewashed logs are the backdrop for this charming getaway's comfy, cottage-style decor. The look is fresh but still warm, thanks to overstuffed seating and textured accessories like the woven wicker coffee table and cane-seated chairs. A few surprises are scattered throughout, including the bead board partition walls and ornamented fireplace that lend a Victorian gingerbread feel to the space. Below, a floor pickled in a harlequin pattern is lively but understated, while the antler lighting fixture above fits right in due to its light coloring. Multipane windows echo the series of archways that lead into the guest quarters from the main house. All together, the space illustrates that log cabin style can be small in scale, light, and fresh.

NEW-AGE RUSTIC

CAREFUL CONSIDERATION, a bit of inspiration, and perhaps some luck will help you find wonderful elements for your contemporary log cabin. When the decor is eclectic, many avenues are open to you when choosing furniture, light fixtures, and other accessories. For example, the talented artisans that are following in the footsteps of yesterday's rustic furniture makers often build pieces with sleek, simple lines. While Victorian-style rustic furniture of the Adirondack Great Camps was layered with bric-a-brac, these pieces are stripped down, putting the beauty of the wood on display. Iron forged into traditional shapes or coaxed into fluid lines can create beautiful lamps, and wood, pottery, and other metals can be found in a wide variety of accessories. If you're overwhelmed by the choices available to you, lean toward elements with an organic feel—those that remind you of nature. Or choose pieces that echo one of the classic cabin styles: Early American, lodge, Western, or Southwestern.

Leafy vines twine around the iron base of this unique desk lamp. Leather lacing and a Native American motif provide graphic impact, while the squared-off shade echoes the shape of the lamp's base. **Manufacturer: Cloudbird.**

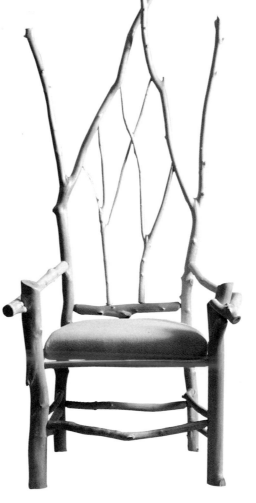

Made from peeled maple branches, this Gothic Revival chair is filled with character and life. **Manufacturer: Daniel Mack Rustic Furnishings.**

Right: *A single forked branch is the only ornament on this pared-down shelf unit. Branches still wearing their bark lend a deep color that's accented by the shelves' planks.* **Manufacturer: Daniel Mack Rustic Furnishings.**

Driftwood, with its silky texture and soft colors, is used to create a free-form table. The lines of the wood recall gentle waves on a lake. **Manufacturer: Daniel Mack Rustic Furnishings.**

This striking entry table is topped with fossil stone and shows the distinctive grain patterns of the juniper tree. **Manufacturer: Custom Furniture by Andy Sanchez.**

Mesquite, the slow-growing tree of the desert, yields interesting grain patterns like those found in the hutch pictured here. Marble and walnut accent the piece's back panels. **Manufacturer: Custom Furniture by Andy Sanchez.**

A classically styled juniper rocking chair is made unique with the addition of angel wing arms. **Manufacturer: Custom Furniture by Andy Sanchez.**

This juniper coffee table echoes the shape of trees sculpted by prevailing winds. **Manufacturer: Custom Furniture by Andy Sanchez.**

ARCHITECTS

Charles Cunniffe Architects
610 E. Hyman Ave.
Aspen, CO 81611
phone 970-925-5590
fax 970-925-5076
info@cunniffe.com
www.cunniffe.com
(9)

Richard Dooley
2996 Grandview Ave. NE
Suite 310
Atlanta, GA 30305
phone 404-365-9311
(82, 83)

The Jarvis Group Architects
P.O. Box 626
511 Sun Valley Road
Suite 202
Ketchum, ID 83340
phone 208-726-4031
fax 208-726-4097
janet@jarvis-group.com
*Mark Deagle, Janet Jarvis, and
Kirk Squier*
(58, 59)

Jerry Locati Architects
402 E. Main St.
Suite 202
Bozeman, MT 59715
phone 406-587-1139
fax 406-587-7369
Jerry Locati
(76, 77)

McMillen Pynn Architecture LLP
P.O. Box 1068
Sun Valley, ID 83353
phone 208-622-4656
fax 208-726-7108
mpynn@sunvalley.net
www.sunvalleyarchitect.com
Mark Pynn, AIA
(118, 119)

Michael Ryan Architects
60 Long Beach Blvd.
Loveladies, NJ 08008
phone 609-494-5000
fax 609-494-4000
(contents, 114, 115)

Miller Architects
Highway 10 W
S. Frontage Road 862
Livingston, MT 59047
phone 406-222-7057
fax 406-222-7372
milleraia@mcn.net
Candace Tillotson-Miller, AIA
(46, 47, 66, 67, 99, back cover)

Otwell Architects
121 E. Goodwin
Prescott, AZ 86303
phone 520-445-4951
fax 520-778-6120
William Otwell
(70, 71)

Jean Steinbrecher
P.O. Box 788
Langley, WA 98260-0788
phone 360-221-0494
fax 360-221-6594
jsa@whidbey.com
(20, 21)

Stephen Dynia Architects
P.O. Box 4356
Jackson, WY 83001
phone 307-733-3766
fax 307-733-1762
sdynia@dynia.com
www.dynia.com
(106, 107)

Strout Architects
85 W. Snow King Ave.
P.O. Box 1251
Jackson, WY 83001
phone 307-733-5778
fax 307-733-1454
contact@stroutarchitects.com
www.stroutarchitects.com
(110, 111)

BUILDERS

Alpine Log Homes, Inc.
118 Main St., P.O. Box 1330
Victor, MT 59875
phone 406-642-3451
www.alpineloghomes.com
(7, 10, 11, 12–13, 36, 37, 92, 93, 114, 115, 116, 117)

Custom Log Homes
P.O. Box 218
Stevensville, MT 59870
phone 406-777-5202
fax 406-777-2738
sales@customlog.com
www.customlog.com
(82, 83)

Hearthstone Homes
120 Carriage Drive
Macon, GA 31210
phone 800-247-4442
fax 912-477-6535
hearthstonehomes@mindspring.com
www.hearthstonehomes.com
(4)

High Country Log Homes
2810 Highway 120
Cody, WY 82414
phone 307-587-3838
fax 307-587-8400
randyolsen@highcountryloghomes.com
www.highcountryloghomes.com
(110, 111)

Lok-N-Logs
Route 12, P.O. Box 677
Sherburne, NY 13460
phone 800-343-8928
fax 607-674-6433
lninfo@loknlogs.com
www.loknlogs.com
(94, 95)

Maple Island Log Homes
5046 S.W. Bayshore Drive
Suite A
Suttons Bay, MI 49682
phone 231-271-4042
fax 231-271-4541
mail@mapleisland.com
www.mapleisland.com
Richard Tuxbury
(front cover, 104–105, 112, 113, 120, 121)

Montana Log Homes
3250 U.S. Highway 93 S
Kalispell, MT 59901
phone 406-752-2992
fax 406-257-7014
David Gray
(56, 57, 68, 69, 98, 108, 109)

Riverbend Timber Framing
P.O. Box 26
Blissfield, MI 49228
phone 517-486-4355
fax 517-486-2056
info@riverbendtf.com
www.riverbendtf.com
(28, 29)

Rocky Mountain Log Homes
1833 Highway 93 S
Hamilton, MT 59840
phone 406-363-5680
fax 406-363-2109
sales@rmlh.com
www.rmlh.com
Mark Moreland
(9, 78, 79, 98, 44–45, 54, 55)

Sisson Log Homes, Inc.
3165 Big Creek Road
Hartford, TN 37753
phone 888-USA-LOGS
fax 423-487-4112
questions@sissonloghomes.com
www.sissonloghomes.com
(16, 17)

Snow Country Construction
8000 Highway 35
Unit 1
Bigfork, MT 59911
phone 408-837-2900
fax 408-837-2902
Mike or Pam Roessman
(40, 41)

Spring Creek Timber Construction
635 County Road 744
Almont, CO 81210
phone 970-641-3367
(22, 23)

Sun Forest Construction
P.O. Box 3396
Sun River, OR 97707
phone 541-593-8204
fax 541-593-6229
www.sforest.com
(58, 59)

Town and Country Cedar Homes
4772 U.S. 131 S
Petoskey, MI 49770
phone 800-968-3178
fax 231-347-7255
info@cedarhomes.com
www.cedarhomes.com
(24, 25, 50, 51)

Unique Log & Timber Works
Box 730
Lumby, BC V0E 2G0
CANADA
phone 250-547-2400
fax 250-547-8888
info@uniquetimber.com
www.uniquetimber.com
(20, 21, back cover)

Yellowstone Traditions
P.O. Box 1933
Bozeman, MT 59771
phone 406-587-0968
fax 406-586-2999
(46, 47, 66, 67, 99, back cover)

DESIGNERS

Dolins Design Studio
555 E. Durant
Aspen, CO 81611
phone 970-925-4472
fax 970-925-4473
dolins@aspeninfo.com
(52, 53)

Dorado Designs, Inc.
4640 E. Sunrise Drive
Tucson, AZ 85718
phone 520-577-1800
fax 520-577-7916
info@doradodesignsinc.com
www.doradodesignsinc.com
(70, 71)

Gandy Peace, Inc.
349 Peachtree Hills Ave. NE
Suite C2
Atlanta, GA 30305
phone 404-237-8681
fax 404-237-6150
www.gandypeace.com
(66, 67, 99)

Lifestyle Interior Design
1925 E. Fourth Place
Denver, CO 80206
phone 303-388-1565
fax 303-388-9067
lifestyle@e.central.com
www.lifestyleinteriordes.com
Sandra Elizabeth Clinger, ASID
(34, 35)

Anna Peavy
206 Thelma Drive
San Antonio, TX 78209
phone 210-822-5504
fax 210-822-3190
(110, 111)

Pump & Circumstance
Route 7, Box 185A
Eureka Springs, AR 72631
phone 501-253-6644
(90, 91)

Slifer Designs
216 Main St., Suite C-100
Edwards, CO 81632
phone 970-926-8200
fax 970-926-8228
info@sliferdesigns.com
www.sliferdesigns.com
Beth Slifer
(58, 59)

Warren Sheets Design
2017 17th St.
San Francisco, CA 94103
phone 415-626-2320
fax 415-626-2770
(40, 41)

MANUFACTURERS

Antler Artistry
134 Pequest Drive
Belvidere, NJ 07823
phone 908-475-5974
fax 908-475-5974
prw@nac.net
www.antlerartistry.com
Paul R. Wiedemann
(63)

Avalanche Ranch Light Company
P.O. Box 31397
Bellingham, WA 98228
phone 888-841-1810
fax 888-841-1812
avalight@avalight.com
www.avalight.com
(102, 103)

Cloudbird
P.O. Box 1322
Twisp, WA 98855
phone 509-997-2348
fax 509-997-5559
(86, 105, 122)

**Custom Furniture by
Andy Sanchez**
1317 Dulcinea
Belen, NM 87002
phone 505-864-2003
fax 505-864-2003
cfasanchez9@aol.com
www.specialtymile.com/
customfurniture
(123)

Daniel Mack Rustic Furnishings
14 Welling Ave.
Warwick, NY 10990
phone 845-986-7293
fax 845-986-9755
rustic@warwick.net
www.danielmack.com
(122)

Hancock & Moore
166 Hancock & Moore Drive
Taylorsville, NC 28681
phone 828-495-8235
fax 828-495-3021
(63)

Livingston Furniture Design
2716 W. 108th Ave.
Hutchinson, KS 67502
phone 620-662-2781
fax 620-663-1122
(87, 127)

Maine Cottage Furniture
P.O. Box 935
Yarmouth, ME 04096
phone 207-846-1430
fax 207-846-0602
info@mainecottage.com
www.mainecottage.com
(102, 103)

**Natalie Fay Linn
Native American Baskets**
4125 S.W. 53rd Ave.
Portland, OR 97221
phone 503-292-1711
fax 503-297-5450
natfaylinn@aol.com
(86, 124)

New West
2811 Big Horn Ave.
Cody, WY 82414
phone 800-653-2391
fax 307-527-7409
newwest@trib.com
www.newwest.com
(64–65, 80, 81)

Plow & Hearth
P.O. Box 5000
Madison, VA 22727
phone 800-627-1712
fax 800-843-2509
info@plowhearth.com
www.plowhearth.com
(42, 43, 126)

Quoizel
590 Old Willets Path
Hauppauge, NY 11788
phone 631-273-2700
fax 631-231-7102
bobbiep@quoizel.com
www.quoizel.com
(42, back cover)

Rustic Furniture
10 Cloninger Lane
Bozeman, MT 59718
phone 406-586-3746
fax 406-582-0844
diane@rusticfurniture.net
www.rusticfurniture.net
(62)

Santos Furniture
2202 Public St.
Cody, WY 82414
phone 888-966-3489
fax 307-527-4407
info@santosfurniture.com
www.santosfurniture.com
(86, 87)

Sleeping Bear Twig Furniture
5711 Rice Road
Cedar, MI 49621
phone 231-228-6633
(contents, 62, 63, 127)

Stickley
Stickley Drive, P.O. Box 480
Manlius, NY 13104-0480
phone 315-682-5500
fax 315-682-6306
www.stickley.com
(13, 42, 43, 125)

Viers Furniture Co.
65 Billman Lane
Livingston, MT 59047
phone 406-222-7564
fax 406-222-2784
www.montanawesternfurn.com
(65, 87, back cover)

Whispering Pines
43 Ruane St.
Fairfield, CT 06430
phone 203-259-5027
fax 203-259-5027
s.panian@snet.net
www.whisperingpines.com
(contents, 45, 62, 63, 89, 102, 124, 125)

PHOTOGRAPHERS

Balance Productions
P.O. Box 956
Bellevue, ID 83313
phone 208-726-6615
balance@svidaho.net
Tim Brown
(118, 119)

Brad Simmons Photography
870 Craintown Road
Perryville, KY 40468
phone 859-332-8400
fax 859-332-4433
brad@bradsimmons.com
www.bradsimmons.com
(contents, 14, 15, 18, 19, 22, 23, 26, 27, 30, 31, 38, 39, 48, 49, 90, 91, 94, 95)

Bryant Photographics
817 S. Higgins
Missoula, MT 59801
phone 406-721-2414
bryant@aol.com
Mark Bryant
(11, 116, 117)

Elijah Cobb Photography
1108 14th St.
Suite 233
Cody, WY 82414
phone 307-587-5218
(86, 87, 105, 122)

F & E Schmidt Photography
488 Quaintance Road
Woodville, VA 22749
phone 540-987-8410
(5, 6)

David Glomb
71340 Estellita Drive
Rancho Mirage, CA 92270
phone 760-340-4455
fax 760-779-1872
d.glomb@worldnet.att.net
(58, 59)

Barry Halkin
Philadelphia, PA
phone 215-236-3922
(contents, 114, 115)

Bobby Hansson
P.O. Box 241
Rising Sun, MD 23704
(122)

James Yochum Photography
1575 N. Rancho Pueblo Court
Tucson, AZ 85712
phone 520-318-4245
fax 520-318-4825
jayochum@aol.com
www.jamesyochum.com
(96, 97)

J.K. Lawrence Photography
14350 Horse Creek Road
Bozeman, MT 59715
phone 406-686-4188
fax 406-686-4190
jklawrence@mcn.net
www.jklawrencephoto.com
(20, 21, back cover)

Conrad Johnson
P.O. Box 8811
Jackson, WY 83002
phone 307-739-4533
(110, 111)

David O. Marlow
421 AABC
Suite J
Aspen, CO 81611
phone 970-925-8882
(52, 53)

Rob Melnychuk
1587 W. Eighth Ave.
Suite 401
Vancouver, BC V6J 1T5
CANADA
phone 604-736-8066
fax 604-736-9339
rob@robmelnychuk.com
www.robmelnychuk.com
(88–89, 100, 101)

Steve Mundinger
475 Brush Creek Road
Aspen, CO 81611
phone 970-923-1055
(9)

Nancie Battaglia Photography
P.O. Box 229
Sweetwood Farms
Lake Placid, NY 12946
phone 518-523-3440
fax 518-523-3501
nbphotog@northnet.org
(60, 61)

Roger Wade Studio, Inc.
P.O. Box 1130
Condon, MT 59826
phone 406-754-2793
fax 406-754-3070
info@rogerwadestudio.com
www.rogerwadestudio.com
Debra Grahl
(front cover, contents, 10, 12–13, 16,
17, 24, 25, 28, 29, 32, 33, 36, 37,
40, 41, 46, 47, 50, 51, 56, 57, 64–65,
66, 67, 68, 69, 70, 71, 72, 73, 74,
75, 76, 77, 80, 81, 82, 83, 84, 85,
98, 99, 104–105, 106, 107, 108, 109,
112, 113, 120, 121, back cover)

Stanley Photography
215 E. Lewis
Livingston, MT 59047
phone 406-222-0900
Larry Stanley
(65, 87, back cover)

OTHER RESOURCES

Adirondack Museum
P.O. Box 99
Blue Mountain Lake, NY 12812-0099
phone 518-352-7311
fax 518-352-7653
www.adkmuseum.org

Buffalo Bill Historical Center
720 Sheridan Ave.
Cody, WY 82414
phone 307-587-4771
www.bbhc.org

Cabin Creek Farm
P.O. Box 208
Summersville, KY 42782
phone 270-299-2226
(contents, 14, 15)

Country's Best Log Homes
11305 Sunset Hills Road
Reston, VA 20190
phone 800-219-1187

Great Lakes Logcrafters Association
24411 Esquire Blvd.
Forest Lake, MN 55025
phone 763-464-3843

International Log Builders Association
P.O. Box 775
Lumby, BC V0E 2G0 CANADA
phone 800-532-2900
fax 250-547-8775
logassoc@junction.net
www.logassociation.org

Lake Placid Lodge
Whiteface Inn Road
Lake Placid, NY 12946
phone 518-523-2700
(60, 61)

Log & Timber Style
7009 S. Potomac St.
Suite 200
Englewood, CO 80112
phone 888-645-7600
fax 303-397-7600
www.logandtimber style.com

Log Home & Timber Frame Expo
phone 888-LOG-EXPO
fax 250-579-9326
info@logexpo.com
www.logexpo.com

Log Home Design Ideas
P.O. Box 500
Missouri City, TX 77459-9917
phone 800-310-7047
fax 281-261-5999
loghomesquest@mcmillencomm.com
www.loghomedesignideas.com

Log Home Plans Online
www.loghomeplansonline.com

Log Homes Council
National Association of
Home Builders
1201 15th St.
Washington, DC 20005
phone 800-368-5242 x576
fax 202-861-2141
pdcrampton@nahb.com
www.loghomes.org

Log Homes Illustrated
P.O. Box 426
Mount Morris, IL 61054-0426

The Log House Builders Association of North America
22203 State Route 203
Monroe, WA 98272
www.premier1.net/~loghouse

Logan Hill Lodge
Logan Road
Gravel Switch, KY 40328
(38, 39)

LogHome. Net
www.loghome.net

Palo Alto Creek Farm
90 Palo Alto Lane
Fredericksburg, TX 78624
phone 800-997-0089
(30, 31)

The Settlement At Round Top
2218 Hartfield Road
Round Top, TX 78954
phone 409-249-5015
(18, 19)

Stock Farm
1883 U.S. Highway 93 S
Hamilton, MT 59840
phone 406-375-1888
(44–45)

Timber Frame Business Council
217 Main St.
Hamilton, MT 59840
phone 800-560-9251
fax 406-375-6401
www.timberframe.org

Timber Framers Guild
P.O. Box 60
Becket, MA 01223
phone 888-453-0879
fax 888-453-0879
info@tfguild.com
www.tfguild.com

Timber Homes Illustrated
P.O. Box 789
Mount Morris, IL 61054

Traditional Building
69A Seventh Ave.
Brooklyn, NY 11217
phone 718-636-0788
fax 718-636-0750
www.traditionalbuilding.com

Western Heritage Center
2822 Montana Ave.
Billings, MT 59101
phone 406-256-6809
www.ywhc.org

The World of Log Homes & Timber Frames
phone 250-376-4290
www.loghomeshow.net

www.loghelp.com
Schroeder Log Home Supply, Inc.
phone 800-359-6614
loghome@loghelp.com

Photo credits:
Front cover: **Roger Wade Studio, Inc./Maple Island Log Homes**
Back cover: **Miller Architects, Candace Miller, AIA/Yellowstone Traditions/Roger Wade Studio, Inc.** (top left); **Quoizel** (top right), **Viers Furniture Co./Stanley Photography/Harley Ferguson Photography** (bottom right); **Unique Log & Timber Works/J.K. Lawrence Photography** (bottom left)
Alpine Log Homes, Inc.: 7, 92, 93; Bryant Photographics, Mark Bryant: 11, 116, 117; Feliciano: 10 (top); Roger Wade Studio, Inc.: 10 (bottom); **Antler Artistry:** 63 (top right); **Avalanche Ranch Light Company:** 102 (bottom right), 103 (bottom right); Brad Simmons Photography: 26, 27, 48, 49; Cabin Creek Farm: Contents (top), 14, 15; Logan Hill Lodge: 38, 39; Lok-N-Logs: 94, 95; Palo Alto Creek Farm: 30, 31; Pump & Circumstance: 90, 91; The Settlement At Round Top: 18, 19; Spring Creek Timber Construction: 22, 23; **Charles Cunniffe Architects/Steve Mundinger:** 9 (top left); **Cloudbird/Elijah Cobb Photography:** 86 (top right), 105, 122 (top right); **Custom Furniture by Andy Sanchez:** 123; **Custom Log Homes/Roger Wade Studio, Inc.:** 82, 83; **Daniel Mack Rustic Furnishings/Bobby Hansson:** 122 (top center, bottom left & bottom right); **Dolins Design Studio/David O. Marlow:** 52, 53; **F & E Schmidt Photography:** 5, 6; **Hancock & Moore:** 63 (top left); **Hearthstone Homes:** 4; **James Yochum Photography:** 96, 97; **The Jarvis Group Architects/David Glomb:** 58, 59; **Lifestyle Interior Design:** 34, 35; **Livingston Furniture Design/Monty Davis:** 87 (top right), 127 (top); **Maine Cottage Furniture:** 102 (bottom left), 103 (top left, top right & bottom left); **McMillen Pynn Architecture LLP, Mark Pynn, AIA/Balance Productions, Tim Brown:** 118, 119; **Rob Melnychuk:** 88–89, 100, 101; **Michael Ryan Architects/Barry Halkin:** Contents (bottom left), 114, 115; **Miller Architects, Candace Miller, AIA/Yellowstone Traditions/Roger Wade Studio, Inc.:** 46, 47, 66, 67, 99; **Montana Log Homes/Roger Wade Studio, Inc.:** 56, 57, 68, 69, 98 (left), 108, 109; **Nancie Battaglia Photography:** Lake Placid Lodge: 60, 61; **Natalie Fay Linn Native American Baskets:** 86 (top left), 124 (top); **New West/Roger Wade Studio, Inc.:** 64–65, 80, 81; **Plow & Hearth:** 42 (bottom left & bottom right), 43 (center), 126 (top); **Quoizel:** 42 (top left), 126 (bottom); **Rocky Mountain Log Homes:** 9 (top right & bottom), 78, 79, 98 (right); L. Hanselman Photography: 54, 55; Stock Farm: 44–45; **Roger Wade Studio, Inc.:** Contents (right center) 12–13, 16, 17, 28, 29, 32, 33, 36, 37, 40, 41, 70, 71, 72, 73, 74, 75, 76, 77, 84, 85, 106, 107; Maple Island Log Homes: 104–105, 112, 113, 120, 121; **Rustic Furniture:** 62 (top); **Santos Furniture/Elijah Cobb Photography:** 86 (bottom), 87 (bottom); **Sleeping Bear Twig Furniture/Don Rutt:** Contents (bottom right), 62 (bottom right), 63 (top center), 127 (center); **Stickley:** 13, 42 (top right), 43 (top left, top center & top right), 125 (center); **Strout Architects/Conrad Johnson:** 110, 111; **Town and Country Cedar Homes/Roger Wade Studio, Inc.:** 24, 25, 50, 51; **Unique Log & Timber Works/J.K. Lawrence Photography:** 20, 21; **Viers Furniture Co./Stanley Photography/Harley Ferguson Photography:** 65, 87 (top left); **Whispering Pines:** Contents (left center), 45, 62 (bottom left), 63 (bottom), 89, 102 (top left, left center & right center), 124 (bottom), 125 (top).